# Politicians
# GASLIGHTING
# Americans

*by*

Dennis Gravelle and Jack Young

Dorrance Publishing Co
585 Alpha Drive
Pittsburgh, PA 15238
Visit our website at *www.dorrancebookstore.com*

ISBN: 979-8-89027-043-6
eISBN: 979-8-89027-541-7

# Contents

# Introduction

Hello, and thanks for picking up this book. Part of the name from our book came from an individual who said Gaslighting Americans would be a good name. We don't remember who it was, so we will say anonymous, but we thank them. That got us thinking, and I had to look up gaslighting, and we found this meaning in the Merriam-Webster Dictionary.

1. "Psychological manipulation of a person usually over an extended period of time that causes the victim to question the validity of their own thoughts, perception of reality, or memories and typically leads to confusion, loss of confidence and self-esteem, the uncertainty of one's emotional or mental stability, and a dependency on the perpetrator
2. the act or practice of grossly misleading someone, especially for one's own advantage."

It immediately hit us that all we needed to do is add 'politician' to the front of the name. Those meanings stood out so much; it's like we were slapped in the face. Politicians gaslight citizens daily and have been doing so for far too long. We decided to name this creation by the people for the people, *Politicians Gaslight Americans*. We feel the name fits exactly with the topics we are covering in these twelve short chapters.

Across this country, we seem to have elite politicians and big corporations telling us they should be trusted and that "We the People" should be little sheep and remain quiet so a new world order can be created. They don't need our input since they already know what we want. Mainstream media programs always want to get the experts' advice, so they get high-profile politicians to talk down to Americans. It is sad because most of America has become brainwashed. That includes Democrat and Republican constituents. Several of us see through the lies and are becoming more vocal. This is a book where you, the citizens of this great country, tell everyone how we really feel about where this country is heading. Politicians should read this and understand that we are fed up with the lack of action from them. This book is easy to read; the chapters are not long enough to bore you. This book is dedicated to all those individuals who took the time to answer the questions I asked over several months.

I am not a writer but did spend time in the United States Army as a photojournalist, writing stories for Soldiers in the New York National Guard and while stationed in Iraq from 2005-06. There was no better job than having Soldiers talk about themselves and the importance of the unit they were assigned to and then telling their story. I was honored and blessed with that opportunity. I thank my fellow Soldiers from the 138th Public Affairs Detachment for making the best of a bad situation, and I especially want to thank the Soldiers from the 172nd Stryker Brigade out of Alaska. The Soldiers of that unit made me feel welcome and safe out on patrol.

"Even though I am educated with a Master of Science degree in leadership with an emphasis in homeland security and emergency management, this really means nothing to anyone else. I say that because many people with degrees think they are better than anyone else, especially our politicians. I may have a degree, but I still get up and go to work every day to a job that I love—security in a hospital. I have good days and bad days, just like everyone else does. Some days I struggle through life, and other days I feel like no one can stop me."

Jack is also not a writer by trade. However, we did put two minds together to complete this book about how people feel. We feel you will enjoy what people have told us about this country. This book isn't for everyone, and that's fine. We tried to find something different, and we believe if you do pick our book up, you will enjoy the comments. We have become a country that people don't even recognize, so we hope these individuals will help inspire others that are also tired of these politicians. One thing we can say about these courageous individuals is that they are not brainwashed.

This book covers current hot topics in America that are sure to affect our future. Basically, this book is by the people, for the people, and shares the opinions of the Soldiers that I interviewed. I am sure that Jack and I will be criticized by some for these topics. We don't care; we must wake people up before we lose our basic rights and freedoms. These fed-up citizens who kindly agreed to be interviewed are Patriots, and without them, we could not have completed this book. Jack and I are just the conduit; everyone who shared their stories made writing this book for all people an amazing and rewarding experience.

This book comes from our hearts and how we feel about the future of America, along with everyone who answered our questions. One thing for sure is that our country has lost its compass, and we need to Stand United to get back on the right course. We feel these two parties are not the answer, and we'll talk about that in this book. We didn't interview any congressional members because we don't trust them. We didn't talk with big corporations because they are just as bad as politicians. No, my friends, this is a book by average people who are fed up with politics and want to see a better America for their families.

We started writing this book in September of 2022, about five weeks before the midterm elections. The election in November 2022, like most elections for Congress, was for control of each congressional house. We felt this is most likely the most important election of our lifetime. Since Joe Biden was elected in our 2020 election, we have seen record inflation, numbers we haven't seen since Jimmy Carter was in office, and that was back in 1976-80. A very long time ago. We have seen gas prices double; 401Ks have tumbled, and everything we buy, such as food, has seemed to triple. We are not in a good economy anymore. Before we begin the hot topic, our first chapter will be a review of historical documents. Please don't skip this part; we want to start everyone on the path to educating themselves because Knowledge is Power.

# About the Authors

Dennis Gravelle was born and raised in upstate New York. After graduation, he joined the United States Air Force to serve his country. His job in the AF was security police where he was stationed in Plattsburgh, NY. He received an honorable discharge and headed on to his next career He then went to work in a County Correctional Facility as a correctional officer where he worked for the next 22 years retiring in 2010. While working full-time in corrections he put himself through the regional police officer school graduating in 2005. He worked part-time in policing until 2016 when he moved out of NY.

After the Twin Towers were destroyed by terrorists on 9/11, he again felt it was his patriotic duty to get back into the military. He joined The NY Army National Guard and worked as a photojournalist serving one tour in Iraq in 2005-06. "Writing stories for Army Soldiers and their companies was a great honor."

In 2016, Dennis moved to South Carolina in the Grand Strand area becoming a full-time police officer. While working this job he finished his Bachelor of Science degree in public safety and emergency management and got his Master of Science in leadership with an emphasis in homeland security and emergency management. "I was burnt out in the policing community after 32 years and being passed over for a promotion I decided to try working in the private sector." Now, he works in the security field and created a new passion with the people he works with. He is also following his passion in waking people up about our country and how we are being ruined by politicians. "People no longer has a voice in politics and are told just to follow politicians. However, they are corrupt and deceitful, and we the people of this country are starting to wake up and fight back. This book is a voice of some of those people. Politicians can't keep us silenced any longer, for we have had enough and are fed up with politics."

I (Jack Young) was born in Brooklyn 1969, a year when man walked on the moon and the Mets won the World Series, what a year to be born! I come from a family of seven and lived my younger years in Moab, Utah. A place of wonder for a young boy who could take his dog and BB gun to go hunting for Thanksgiving dinner, where I rode ponies bare back, where wild horses roamed the valley, where I helped put up our own electric pole and dug our own septic tank, where life was wonderful for a young boy. Kind of like Tom Sawyer. Then we moved back to New York, and I earned my associate in science and joined the NYPD at age twenty. In 1999 when I was 30, I became a sergeant. I worked the day of 9/11/2001, a horrific day that I will never forget or ever be able to completely explain. I developed my own oil delivery business and then retired in South Carolina.

I married my wife in 1990 and had four wonderful children with her. Our eldest Jack is a young man who is immersed in the Special Olympics. He is not only a participant (with many medals) he also helps finance the organization with fundraisers. Jack is involved with assisting with the recordings, and he runs the South Carolina Facebook page, "United States Constitutional Group." Sean Patrick is our next son, the father of our beautiful granddaughter. He was stationed in Germany serving for five years in the Army. We are very proud of him and thank him for the sacrifices he made while serving our country and fighting for our freedom. We are looking forward to his return home. Our third son is Brandon, one of South Carolina Fire Department's bravest. He is working towards his certification as a paramedic. Brandon puts a lot of effort and pride into his advancements. We have two rambunctious grandsons from him and his wife, they are such a joy. After three boys, you can imagine our excitement when we had our baby girl, our princess Meagan. She works at a DNA lab in Connecticut. I wouldn't be surprised if she found a cure for something important one of these days. If you tell this girl, "You can't," she comes back with, "Oh, yeah? Watch me!" and then does it. She loves the city and the hustle and bustle it provides. As her parents, we hope someday she settles down south with us.

Today, my wife Missy and I live in a resort in South Carolina, living our dream. After thirty-one years of marriage, I couldn't love her any more than I did the day I married her. She has given me the support and courage to follow my dreams and help me make them come true. That includes my and Dennis's idea to create the United States Constitutional Group Podcast "Meet at the Tavern," developing our website "Fed up with politics" and writing this book. As my parents installed strong passion and hard work, it gave me the confidence to move forward with my political devotion to making representatives follow our Declaration of Independence and the U.S. Constitution. This needs to be followed for our generations to come so that their freedom is never infringed upon, and they can live in the America we grew up in.

# Chapter 1

# Historical Writings that built the United States of America

Let's start off with two historical documents that helped create the United States. We always tell our listeners on our Facebook live show called Stand United with Jack and Dennis, that "KNOWLEDGE IS POWER" and that people should research for themselves what we talk about that day. The more you know about a subject, the better you can handle yourself in a debate, or just a conversation in general. There is no better place to start than by reviewing important information from the forming of our country.

Take a moment or two and head to the back of the book and read the ***Declaration of Independence.***

And, while you're at it, why not look at the United States Constitution, also in the back of the book.

# Chapter 2

# "Our Economy"

With inflation almost at a forty-year high with higher prices throughout this economy, do you feel better off today than you did 3 years ago?

In January 2020, Joe Biden was elected our 46th President of the United States of America. This was a contested election that started the big divide in our country. Republicans and Democrats started hating each other, and that was just the beginning. Our 45th President, Donald Trump, claimed that the election was stolen and that the electoral votes should be cast out because the Democratic machine had rigged the election. That has never been proven and most likely never will be. We agree that we had cheating in that election, but it was on both sides. However, people could not move forward. We do know this—just before President Trump left office we had a great economy. People were saving money and taking vacations again thanks to easing Covid restrictions. Gas prices were at the lowest prices we'd seen since the 80s. The economy was thriving, and people were starting to get back into a healthy routine. We believe the middle class was starting to feel good about America. I (Dennis) know having a great economy was the sole reason why I bought a 2020 Toyota Tacoma. This was my dream vehicle I had wanted for twenty years and finally, I could justify the purchase, due to lower gas prices. Filling the tank up was reasonable and affordable. It cost under forty dollars to fill my gas tank. I was living well. January 20, 2020, was when it all changed.

So, what happened? you ask. Plain and simple, in layman's terms "Joe Biden was elected President." On the campaign trail, he told every one of us that he would be the most progressive president to hold the highest office in the land. We don't know who in their right mind would vote for that kind of president, but they say he received 81 million votes. Trump, on the other hand, received about 75 million. When conducting a search on the internet it states there were just over 168 million voters. I find it hard to believe that over 90 percent of registered voters voted during this election, when the most a presidential election had ever earned previously was 58 percent of voters, in 2008.

Right now, those numbers seem sketchy but that doesn't matter currently. On January 20th, the first day in office for our new president, he stopped drilling permits for oil companies and stopped the Key Stone Pipeline (KSP) from being completed. Many citizens were employed by KSP and immediately lost their livelihoods. Biden had no plan in place for these laid-off workers to get new jobs. He had no solution for helping people in need. He didn't care, he wanted to move ahead with his agenda to transform America. Instead of being a uniter as he promised during his campaign, he was and still is the divider of this great country.

Personally, I am doing alright. I had to cut back on vacations, don't go out to eat like I used to, and mostly travel only back and forth to work to save money on gas. I was going to buy a house earlier this year but when I looked at these houses, they were priced way out of my range. The housing market in Myrtle Beach was booming and construction companies were building new developments all over the south strand, but average working people could not afford them. I believe there are a few indicators that the economy is tanking, and I really don't see any relief soon. The first indicator for me is high prices, which puts everyone in a tough spot. With higher gas prices comes higher food costs for everything we buy, from consumable goods to merchandise. With my question we asked about being better off now than three years ago, I received some great comments. Listed below are several responses from individuals. We did try to get back to most people who commented by a short answer or liking their response on Facebook. America will get to see what people are talking about and something our politicians should read, so they can see that they are the ones causing this mess. People are talking and they are fed up with the way things are going. Let's begin.

*Please note that all quotes in this book are unedited and uncorrected, for authenticity.*

**MaLady Alonda**: *No, I do not, everything is 2 to 3 times more expensive. I ride in a big rig, traveling this country delivering loads of different foods across this country. Things are getting scarce out here; loads are fewer and fewer. The cost to haul the loads is way more expensive, but the pay for hauling the loads is getting cheaper. Inflation is growing at rapid speed, as production of product declines. It's about to get worse by next week from my understanding of what's happening. Prices will not go down any time soon, as too many of our processing plants keep blowing up and burning down, along with other causes of shutting them down."*

She knows first-hand that prices like gas are soaring way out of control and it's getting tougher for all truck drivers. We have all heard about the railroad workers who are threatening to strike over wages and benefits. Being that the union workers supported this democratic administration; in return the White House is trying to negotiate a 24% pay raise. There are several special interest individuals who have invested in the railroad. This truck driver will tell you exactly what that will do for her business. We are sure this government is trying to take away their livelihood, just like they did on day one with the Keystone Pipelines workers.

*Bobbie:* *"Three years ago I could pay my bills, for the most part, and still have money for essentials like food, med, necessities, and put gas in my vehicle. Now, even though I earn more then I did 3 years ago, I can't afford to pay my bills never mind have any extra left for everything else. The cost of everything has gone up: utilities, gas, rent, food, everything. So now I struggle to find a way to pay my bills never mind have anything left over for the rest. I would love for someone to tell me what the solution is. I went from working less than 40 hours a week and being able to get by, to working 50 to 60 hours a week and still not bringing in enough for my expenses."*

*Floyd:* *"I am not doing near as well as I was 3 years ago. Thanks to the DemoRATS. Thanks Joe you POS."*

*David:* *"3 years ago*

*gas 1.89 in Louisiana, Food, building materials, clothing, etc. Now everything doubled and tripled.*

*racism, hatred, lies, conspiracies, and hoax's perpetrated by democrats and media has made unrest throughout the nation.*

*The Green New Deal when implicated will bring more problems to the people, more than the entire past 200 plus years of financial burden.*

*The democrats are always experimenting with the American population , to see how far they can get their ideologies injected into the nation, sense Lyndon Johnson with welfare programs that really don't work, public schools an experiment of failure , the experiment of letting criminals out and no bail will take a toll on the public, the blm , antifa and the woke generation is also a bad experiment will leave a lot to think about!*

*The electric vehicles will prove to be a burden on the middle class and poor, only the rich can afford them and would just be a toy to play with, I predict that now is not the time for this and it will fail the automobile industry will lose billions along with the American taxpayer another failed experiment.*

*The experiment of Solyndra by the Obama administration even though they were warned of its possible failure went ahead with it anyway and poof 500 million bucks of our money wasted!*

*nothing has gotten any better except when Trump administration was in charge it seems to me that from the time of president Jimmy Carter , to Obama and now Biden the public has a short memory of the failed experimenting they have performed on the American public their system of relentlessly using us as Guinea pigs instead of solving problems with actual hard work and common sense, not to say the republicans faired any better.*

*were we better off 3 years ago the answer is absolutely not, we did well under Regan and Trump a thing the public soon forgets especially electing what we have now, a failing experiment of a political nightmare, that will take a long time to recover from. A lesson learned maybe yes, maybe no."*

At this present time in our history electric vehicles are still in the beginning stages. the things we see wrong with them right now number one they don't get very many miles uncharged so going on a long vacation or working out of your car like a real estate broker just wouldn't be feasible for those people. Next, they just cost too much money right now, some costing more than a gas vehicle. With the way inflation has been in the last two years, only people making lots of money can afford these cars. They are not for average people especially for people living on the minimum wage. We are sure you can buy cheaper electric vehicles, but how reliable will they be. Hybrids still run on gasoline, not exclusively on electric, and when you change the batteries, you might as well just get a new car because they cost in the thousands of dollars too. Technology will improve in the future and maybe someday electric vehicles will be commonplace here in America, that time is not now. These electric vehicles are not an experiment but a further push to the administrative state working towards socialism, fascism, and later, communism. We all remember a time when Alexandra Ocasio Cortez stood on the steps of the Capital Building telling us about this Green New Deal. We all thought she was a joke, but who's the joke on now? We are heading in that direction.

***Glenn:*** *"No, not better today than three years ago. I'm disabled and on SSDI (Social Security Disability Income) ...with no extra income and the loss of my wife's job do to it being closed...it's very difficult to make ends meet...the wife got another job...but pays much less then her old one... medical cost continues to increase...good Drs are harder to find.... gas is impossible. It's too expensive so must stay closer to home when we used to be able to shop around for best prices now it's not worth it.....even had to cut meds because they are too expensive.....can't continue to maintain things at this rate much longer...we need a change and change now"*

We feel that finding a doctor will get harder and harder because this democrat party wants to introduce socialized medicine just like Canada gives to their people. American citizens have worked hard at their jobs to get private medical insurance like we did when we belonged to a union. Politicians want to take away your choice of what doctor you want to use unless you are one of the lucky ones to have private health insurance. Is that fair for the hard-working Americans of this country? We've heard people today talk about how they go to Urgent Care, and they're sent away to go to the emergency room because the doctor doesn't want to see any patients, unless you have access to a Preferred Provider Organization. The citizens on Medicaid find it harder to use local Urgent Care centers. Several states are even taking benefits away like my employers did to me (Dennis) when I worked in NY. We both work in a local hospital now here in South Carolina and we have had patients walk in and stated that they just came from a Urgent Care. Do you see where we are going here? We're living in a sad world. And we are on a rapid decline.

We don't blame one party for this healthcare mess. No, we blame it on both parties (democrat and republican) for this broken system, but they are too stubborn to work together to find common ground so we the people are the ones left suffering.

***Anonymous:*** *"No. I do not! Everything costs more and seems like everything goes up from week to week. Groceries. Gas. Utilities."*

***Gregory:*** *"Tragically this is the worst economic crisis I've lived. The Democratic ideology has lost its way a long time ago. The last good Democratic politician was JFK! America needs to get back to its root values under God's Blessings and guidance. Brandon is just a talking head for the corrupt string pullers who seem to have a never-*

*ending seat in office. Term limits for all elected government officials would be a great start. We need to dump the Democrats in the upcoming elections!"*

We agree with Gregory that John F, Kennedy was the last true Democrat, but just like everyone else he had his faults, he loved this country went to war for that cause. We need people to understand that the true swamp it is not our elected officials, the swamp of the United States government is the unelected bureaucracies.

**Evelyn:** *"I feel worse off than I did 3 years ago! The Biden administration is guilty of*

    *01. Not closing out border southern border*

    *02. Allowing migrants to enter our country without being thoroughly vetted*

    *03. Allowing migrants to enter our country without being tested for Covid*

    *04. Allowing migrants to enter our country without a Covid vaccine*

    *05. Closing the Keystone XL pipeline*

    *06. Not allowing grilling on America soil*

    *07. Baby formula shortage*

    *08. Inflation being over a forty year high*

    *09. Pulling out of Afghanistan with full knowledge of leaving the Taliban an extreme terrorist in charge*

    *10. War on Police*

    *11. War on our children*

    *12. Not keeping Murderers in prison"*

**John:** *"No, I am worse off can't even rent a 1 bedroom apartment."*

**Joanne:** *"No way, the Democrats want us to depend on the government for everything, that's socialism and that's what they want."*

**Pam:** *"Of course not. I'm actually afraid awaiting this administration's next moves to destroy the economy and America."*

**Mary:** *"None of us are better off today other than those who profited from the C19 (Covid-19) crap & all the lucrative Chinese deals. The only way to fix the problem is to clean house in DC! Elect constitutionalists who want to save our country & actually serve our nation, not profit financially from it.*

We have two ways that we can clean up D.C. The first one is going to the voting booth and vote these corrupt politicians out of office. The next way is term limits. These politicians of today will never vote for term limits on themselves, they have too much power and they will never give that up voluntarily. We have read several articles that have stated that we're very close to an Article V State Convention regarding term limits but we need more than just that to real in these tyrants in Washington. We believe that politicians should have special bank accounts that are not tied into the stock market. we must realize and understand that these politicians are getting rich from the laws they passed. Article V of the United State Constitution says this:

"The Congress, whenever two-thirds of both Houses shall deem it necessary, shall propose Amendments to this Constitution, or, on the Application of the Legislatures of two-thirds of the several States, shall call a Convention for pro-posing Amendments, which in either Case, shall be valid to all Intents and Purposes, as Part of this Constitution, when ratified by the Legislatures of three-fourths of the several States, or by Conventions in three fourths thereof, as the one or the other Mode of Ratification may be proposed by the Congress; Provided that no Amendment which may be made prior to the Year One thousand eight hundred and eight shall in any Manner affect the first and fourth Clauses in the Ninth Section of the first Article; and that no State, without its Consent, shall be deprived of its equal Suffrage in the Senate."

These next comments are from people who stated they are doing better today.

***Becky:*** *"Yes, I do feel better. My mental health is worth the higher prices which, of course, have NOTHING to do with the current administration."*

***Jeff:*** *"I am absolutely better off now than 3 years ago. This is in large part due to having started my own company 5 years ago and it has grown every year since.*

*I can also thank wage stagnation for providing me with the motivation to start my own company in the first place. Had I continued to receive raises after 20 years in the industry (hvac) then I wouldn't have been motivated enough to start my own."*

***Anonymous:*** *"I feel better because I, have the knowledge of who and what's behind it all, if we quit sitting on our butts and pushed these corporations with boycotts, they'd soon drop prices.*

*Hey big oil, you're making billions per quarter, maybe we dump your subsidies since you don't really need them now do you."*

For those of you who feel you are better off today, in this economy we believe you are not telling the full story. Unless you are making millions, we really don't think this economy is good for anyone. Higher prices will affect every part of the business you own. That only means you must charge more for the business you provide and that in turn hurts the consumer. Most American citizens just like the ones above are struggling to make it in this economy. When we were reading them, it made me feel sad that in a country like ours, we have politicians on the inside trying to destroy us. They have created the worst situation with our economy since the late 1970s. Biden's Building Back Better has turned into a fiasco. Right now, we are in a two-prong attack with this government (predominately on the left) to rid American citizens of our freedoms and a republic form of government. We need to start thinking about our prosperity.

Another indicator for me is our stock market. People are losing thousands of dollars in their retirement saving such as a 401K. We were up over 30,000 on the stock exchange last year, but high inflation and fears of a recessions are hurting our people who rely on a higher market to earn them a decent retirement savings. A retired State Trooper from New Jersey by the name of John told me he lost 100,000 dollars in the stock market and he is not alone. I (Dennis) have never dabbled with the stock market; I don't understand it and would get too agitated if I lost as much money as these people. Again, it doesn't feel right that someone would lose so much because of what one man did as president. Here are some comments from a few other people in his same position.

*Tina:* "*I've lost 25-30% of my retirement income since Biden took office.*"

*Gary:* "*Where do I start? 3 years ago, My 401k was booming up 25%. Today it's down 21%. The country is so divided to the point that no one listens or even cares what the other side   says. Where are all the people that want a full-time job with benefits? I know your wallet can't be healthier unless you're a lottery winner!!! 3 years ago, America had some common sense.*"

*Pam:* "*No, I do not. Grocery shopping today, a twelve pack of soft drinks has gone from $5.00-$9.00, a box of cereal is now $7.00. My husband's retirement account stayed stable during covid; it's now lost $35,000! Biden is killing this country fast, if we don't regain Congress, this country is gone forever!*"

**David:** *"Dennis Gravelle I lost over $250,000 in investments since Biden took office. That enough for you? Inflation and gas prices certainly don't help either."*

Most people living and working here in the United States cannot afford to place additional money into the stock market. Hell, most of our citizens live paycheck to paycheck and can barely afford to put gas in their vehicles to get them back and forth to work. Imagine what a family of four is going through today, with high rent prices, food, medicine, and maybe baby formula and diapers. We assure you it is not pretty. We hope for the sake of people like those above they will be able to weather the storm. We really have no clue when this economy is going to get better; however, we still pray that it will happen sooner than later.

The last indicator that we are heading for disaster is inflation, which has become a huge issue for the Biden administration. In January 2021 just before taking office, inflation was stable at 1.4 percent. Interest rates were low so people could borrow money to expand their business or even complete work on their houses. Instead of trying to bring inflation down, Biden has pushed his progressive agenda through Congress making the problem worse than it could have been. The inflation stood at 8.2 percent and has moved very little since Biden was elected. Just look at some of the prices that were increased thanks to rising inflation. Gas has gone up 45 cents across the country. Energy costs have gone through the roof, rising 24.5 percent, so heating your home this year may be a challenge, especially this winter. Airfares have flown away, costing travelers over 24 percent more to reach their destination. What it comes down to is that inflation erodes purchasing power. Just ask yourself this question: What percentage of a pay raise did you get from your employer last year, or even this year? If it wasn't 8 percent or better, you are falling behind in this economy. They also call inflation a hidden tax because the extra taxes you pay on everything you buy goes to the federal government. That is used to fund this administration towards progressive policies. We believe we already pay too much in taxes, but you can answer that for yourself. For this chapter I will leave you with these quotes:

**Vic:** *"I have no money, just paying taxes and bills."*
**Robert:** *"The economy is getting ready to crash thanks to the President"*

We totally agree with that statement and want to add that most of our politicians are also to blame. Unless something is done to keep this president in check, we the people must act. We are part of the checks and balances on our government, so we must do our part and head to the voting both every federal, state, and local election that comes up. That brings us to Chapter 3.

# Chapter 3

# "Our Voting Fiasco"

Why should we vote?

When a candidate runs for office and wants your vote what qualities are you looking for?

We were just a few weeks away from the midterm elections of 2022. We believe all of us have qualities that are good and bad. As a politician you should have more good qualities, though. We don't see that in many of our elected members in Congress. So, we wanted to see what people look for in a candidate and to show people how important it is to get out and vote. These past two years have been hard on American citizens. We have seen a great economy with very low inflation and low gas prices become an economy we don't even recognize anymore. We must admit, we were all caught blindsided when Joe Biden won the presidential election. We thought Trump was a shoo-in against a career politician who barely left his bunker.

Why did that happen? We ask ourselves daily and most people on the republican side will tell you the democrats cheated their way to winning that election, and democrats tell us republicans are unpatriotic and don't believe in democracy and are election deniers. There are family members that don't even talk anymore because they believe the hype these two parties throw at us 24 hours a day, through news and internet. Voting constituents don't know who to believe anymore, except the ones who are brainwashed, for they will always be followers. The rest of us are waking up to the games politicians play. A game they have played well for the last 40 years. These career politicians want we the people to believe they know better than us. They tell us who to vote for, what laws should be written and who we should send campaign funds to.

Ah, but we the people we're currently seeing through the games that they play oh so well. People started to wake up, coming out of their shell, standing together as Patriots once did when our country was formed. People were fed up with politicians, still are and want their country back, but don't really know what we can do to get our government where it belongs, and that is back with we the people. This is our country; our government and the timing has never been better to get involved now. There are several ways for us to help in getting our government back, and the first one is voting. This right was given to us in the Constitution of the United States.

Please remember, voting isn't just our right but our duty! It has become our duty since we the constituents are the fourth check and balance of this government. There are three separate branches of government that refuse to be a part of those checks. Therefore, we must rise above them and be the major check and balance for this out-of-control government.

Amendment XV was passed by Congress on February 26, 1869. Ratified February 3, 1870.

SECTION 1. states: "The right of citizens of the United States to vote shall not be denied or abridged by the United States or by any State on account of race, color, or previous condition of servitude."

That is not a privilege but a right that we the people need to honor. Several of us for one reason or another have given up on this right and don't even vote anymore. That can't happen anymore. We are sure that many citizens feel the same as the people we are about to mention. Voting is important and there are many individuals who just lost confidence and have never voted. They don't believe the system is fair and believe change is needed. The one important piece we want to mention is that we need to vote to be heard.

*Cherie:* "*Anyone who doesn't feel voting is important is part of the problem!! Not voting, whether you feel your vote doesn't count or because of election fraud ... simply means that you're complicit with the corruption and don't really care about the state of this Nation!*"

*William:* "*Voting is an important part of having your voice heard. If one doesn't vote, then one doesn't get to complain about the results. You didn't use your voice when it mattered.*"

*John:* "*It's vital that we vote in this election! Our freedom is on the ballot! If you love American and you love the opportunities you have here, then we must vote and we must vote RED All the way down the ballot. The alternative is Communism, just by their policies alone.*"

*Jim:* "*Voting is important because the people hold the power in a constitutional republic like ours to hold our political representatives accountable for their choices (on our behalf) while they are in an office of public service. If we don't exercise our own civil virtues and hold our political representatives accountable then it is our fault that we have a corrupt political environment as much as it is the politicians whom choose to be corrupt and cash in on bribes and sell out the best interests of their constituency A dutiful voter (see: 98% reelection rate whilst actually having a 20% approval rating ) that is voting on party lines does not really exercise civil virtues and is not to be confused with a diligent and well informed voters that exercises their civil virtues by holding accountable our politicians."*

**Phoenix:** *"My posted comments when voters' pamphlets arrived in my area : Whether you know it or not, friend, YOU are in the WAR of a LIFETIME!!! Unprecedented times?! Y E S . . .you've seen it, you've heard it - you've FELT IT. The war is upon us. Complacency in your life allows our free American Republic to slip away moment by moment…... SOMETHING WE CANNOT ALLOW! VOTERS PAMPHLETS HITTING YOUR HOMES, today (and through the weekend), Cowlitz County!!!!! Get it. Find it. USE IT. I am SO SICK of hearing good, morally sound, hardworking people say, "I'm not going to vote, because my vote doesn't count!" - OR - "The left just cheats anyway! So, it doesn't matter!" I call BULLSH!T - so just STOP. HERES THE TRUTH: Those who oppose truth and justice have ALREADY WEAPONIZED THEIR VOTES AGAINST YOU. Can you REALLY AFFORD to put down your sword <vote> on this one?*

*Think about what's at stake here: *Your freedom *Your choices *Your children lives and legacy *Your businesses, houses, & way of life * pretty much EVERYTHING YOU HOLD DEAR If you feel you are morally sound, work hard, & love AMERICA - YOU MUST VOTE!!!!!! There is NO DOUBT that WE ARE AT WAR Stop with the excuses. . Pick up your sword <vote> and FIGHT the battles YOU CAN!!!!! VOTING is the very LEAST you can do…..get on it. "*

**Anonymous**: *"Voting is a privilege that I exercise in every election. If you don't vote, you sacrifice your opportunity to use your voice. However, it would appear that the government is currently utilizing the American taxpayers to purchase votes. Something must change; we have a corrupt government that seems to feel the American citizen works for them instead of the way it was intended to be. I will continue to vote and hooper that it will make a positive difference. God bless America.*

*A right cannot be taken away. I feel privileged to have the opportunity to vote, it matters to me."*

***Emanon:*** *"Because we are supposed to be a self-governing nation and for far too long have allowed others to take control. It's to the point now where the politicians believe themselves to be completely separate from the people and seek to rule not govern. We can only change that by taking the power back. And at this point it is not going to be easy"*

***Julie:*** *"Voting is important to make sure our opinion is counted. It is extremely important to me, and equally important is that only those eligible to vote do vote. That's where it gets complicated with ballet harvesting, voting @ facilities where help is needed to cast that vote. So, to be fair voting practices are equally important as the actual vote cast."*

***Vince:*** *"Voting is a good thing for all American citizens to participate in and they should be kept fair. lately I suspect tampering, corruption and buying votes. dead people can't vote neither can non-citizens. elections should be fair. my confidence in the system has been shaken."*

***Chuck:*** *"Voting, in general, is our Constitutional input into Government operations. Specifically, it our voice to the overall health of the Nation."*

***Salvatore P:*** *"It is our civic duty to vote in each and every election millions of Americans have served, and thousands have died giving us the right to vote."*

***A.J. Ward:*** *A citizen of the great experiment of Democracy has the most important responsibility in civilization as a voter. All eligible citizens have the right and responsibility of selecting our representatives for all offices, local and national. Organized voter suppression is the greatest crime against Democracy."*

***Kiki:*** *"Never voted in my life. Now? I'm considering it. The direction we're heading is insane. I would vote red (obviously.)"*

***Beth:*** *"It's an illusion to make us think we have any power.... especially on presidential and upper levels. Focus on your community and county and sheriff. Your vote for a good constitutional sheriff is what matters."*

***Alexa:*** *"I vote because neither my grandparents nor my parents were born with the right to vote without having to jump through excessive hoops. I also vote because I have grandchildren (especially my granddaughters) and I want them to have MORE rights than I have not less!"*

***Maria:*** *"We still have the opportunity to vote fraud and all! But we must Vote! It's our constitutional duty and right! We put these idiots in power! Please at least* *know who you're voting for? Your life, our lives will be run by the idiots you choose! So, Vote responsibly! Save the USA 😎 from those who are working so hard at destroying us from within!"*

Voting rights are not restrictive as politicians want us to believe. All states have voter laws in place. You should follow the law of your state. If it requires you to get an identification, go get one. There is no excuse saying I can't get one. Your local sheriff's department or Department of Motor Vehicles can and will issue anyone a state identification card. Polling stations are placed in a community where everyone can make it to vote. If you are elderly or need assistance, ask someone to pick you up to get you there. For everyone else who is a healthy individual, walk down to the polling station like they used to do when cars hadn't been invented. People are tired of hearing excuses as to why they can't vote, people are tired of hearing that voting is racist. People are tired of hearing that democrats are cheats, republicans are racist, making any excuse as to why their candidate might not win. Stop listening to these politicians and the parties they belong to. They are corrupt and downright deceitful. We have no use for career politicians anymore in this country. When a political candidate asks for your support, ask them the tough question that you need to hear, and if they give you an answer you don't like, tell them to move on. Don't let these parties dictate to you that you will support this person or that person. Make your own determination. When there are primaries, parties need to remain neutral and let the people decide.

The 2022 midterm election was probably one of the most important elections we as a country have seen in our history. Did we as citizens want to continue with this president's progressive agenda, or do we want to say, Whoa, we need to slow down. We, the voting people have not used our power wisely. We have the power to say who gets elected and when it's time for them to go. Our government is supposed to have checks and balances that would stop this tyranny, that's why there are three separate branches of government. Right now, those balances are gone, so it leaves we the people with the most important decision of our lifetime—being that check and balance to stop the insanity.

The last three weeks we the people had to think about the candidates on party line ballots and think long and hard about what they represent. Did they reflect your values, did they care about the issues that you care about, and more importantly, do they believe in the constitution? Do the right thing and use what our constitution gives us. People were excited to cast their vote and were proud they did.

It is time for citizens to ensure that we have a country that represents everyone in this society, and we accomplish that by looking to politicians with ideals that we believe will look out for our best interests. Here are quotes from different folks, and we thank them for their honesty.

When leaving the Constitutional Convention one lady asked Benjamin Franklin, "What kind of government did you make us?" He informed her, "A republic type government, if you can keep it." By not taking your duty to vote seriously and with dedication, you are proving politicians right when they say, "Do as we say; we know better." This should be enough reason to start doing your due diligence in understanding who you are placing in office when voting.

*Sheila:* "*Integrity* ✓ *morals* ✓ *honesty* ✓ *Backbone.* ✓ *Proven records of all qualities*"

*Gina:* "*Personally, I feel that the people that get vetted are not the ones we need as a country. The two parties both bring up a lot of issues that not only distract us but segregate us. I feel we should vote anyways but we need to choose leaders that walk a moral path. Not a religious path per say but no cheating, lying, stealing, or using loopholes to stay on top or get out of trouble. A leader that considers all human life precious and equal. One that cares about our environment because if we kill this world, we are really up da poo creek with no paddle. I'm disgusted by what I see in the world, people quoting the freedom of speech but twisting it to say it's ok to be verbally cruel to others. Freedom of speech was about protecting people from persecution or worse when not agreeing with the people in charge. It's a self-absorbed world for yet we have the sentience to rise above all the bs and actually care about each other especially the less fortunate. To all the winners in the world that look down on "losers" as they call them: there would be no winners without losers and all people can fill a role best suited to them which kind of ditches those classifications except for in sports* "

*Diane:* "*Well, let's be clear, Dennis…. there is no easy solution…. but we are a nation that has totally lost its moral compass, and truthfully, it will be difficult to come back from that. I would appreciate a politician who is not bought…. but one who truly believes in the Constitution and will fight like hell to defend it.*"

*Gena:* "*A supporter of the constitution. Second amendment gun rights. Integrity if possible. Pro Life. Republican not a RINO. Close Borders .All of this is difficult to know and until they are in office, they can say anything ... their past political stances... and if it changes for votes."*

**Kelli:** *"Loyalty to our Republic. Uphold the constitution. America first. Good morals. Willing to fight for what is right. Mean what they say and say what they mean."*

**Mary:** *"Proven intelligence, deep understanding of the Constitution, leader with a middle-class agenda, progressive mindset, no trace of scandal, a desire to deconstruct Citizens United, agenda to add more judges to the Supreme Court, agenda to tax large corporations who shamefully avoid their fair share."*

**Martha:** *All that encompasses good American values, someone who understands the difference between a man and a woman, and someone who doesn't agree with the sexualization of our young children."*

**Ron:** *"Do they know what system of government we are guaranteed under the constitution? Do they know why oaths are required? Do they know what perjury is, and what the penalties are for committing it? Do they have a full and accurate understanding of the definition of treason? Do they know and appreciate who it is they work for and who they are accountable to? Can they give a cogent reason why people should support and vote for them?"*

**Rob:** *"Their adherence to the constitution. Specifically, the 2nd amendment."*

**Gary:** *"Platform/policies that reflect an adherence to the Constitution and in no way purports any issue that would undermine the Constitutional Republic. Being a Biblical Christian is of course strongly desired with a dedication to oppose any "Rights" that violate "the Laws of Nature and of Nature's God" as the opening paragraph of the Declaration of Independence set as the premise for how "Rights" were to be "entitled."*

**Beverly:** *"I look for Core Values. A) Constitutional Conservative* 😎 *Law and Order C) Protects Life  D) Smaller Government    The list is long"*

**Sandy:** *"Courage. Someone who understands the various ways the left is undermining this great nation thru social and cultural issues. Someone who is authentically in support of limited govt-reigning in bureaucracy Someone who understands that my body belongs to me as a gift from God and that medical experimentation and/or coercion is NOT OK. It's a slippery slope. It's why the Nuremberg code exists. Someone who understands that we must protect the innocence of our children and Sexualization MUST STOP. I would ask them if they've taken a constitution class and what do they love most about America? What do THEY believe* *is the most dangerous way America is being attacked? I would want them to explain DEI/CRT/Intersectionality and implicit bias."*

*"If they understood the gravity of the cultural subversion undermining this nation, if they revered American Exceptionalism, if they understood our constitution, if they understood body autonomy or how our children are being attacked thru Sexualization and indoctrination, if they understood the faith filled roots of this nation, if they understood how important America was in furthering the great commission, and understood the importance of America as a world power in this nation-I'm guessing they would have been better able to protect this great nation.*

*We don't need more laws; we need legislators who will protect the idea that objective truth exists*

*And truth be told we citizens along with the church have failed to keep watch as well.*

*We were complacent handing over our liberty to those who've had a planned attack against America for years and years.*

*We essentially gave it away.*

*But some of us rose up. We tried to explain the vaccine injuries. We were ignored because the medical community knew better.*

*We tried to explain the dangers of social justice which seek to dismantle our form of govt and elevate relativism over truth-it was too complicated they wouldn't listen.*

*And schools? And the churning out of little Marxists? I can't believe there is not more outrage from government leaders*

*The truth is, everything is in place, tyranny is being advanced, we (America and other great nations) are poised to move into globalism - America will have to be weak in all areas to accomplish that."*

*"I believe we should all be remnants for God and for truth until the end. Regardless of if we win or lose. But truthfully, I feel it's too late for man to affect change. The spiritual battle is great, and it is my opinion that the only way to correct this trajectory is for God to intervene. So, prayer is essential*

*And yet, we weren't promised a revival right now.*

*We're within the last days of one generation prophetically for-told about Israel's birth as a nation.*

*The events of scripture feel as if they're lining up.*

*Yet we must persevere. Giving up is not an option"*

*"Also, yes, our govt is corrupt. Yes, we have a uniparty. Our republican Caucuses work to advance republicanism but what is a republican?*

*Republicans (of which I am one) have no way to uphold the platform. Nothing in our bylaws allows us to vet, rate and we rarely censure. Our bylaws exist to maintain party politics. That's it.*

*So, the platform, which rests on the constitution, is nothing more than virtue signaling IF people read it.*

*But sadly, even the platform is now tired and not bold enough. Too much has changed since 2016 and the language of the platform must call for courage, strength, principle, character. We must boldly address gender and sexuality, body autonomy and the medical industrial complex, the social justice attacks by Progressives that seek to undermine our form of govt, the attacks on our youth, the attack on Life, truth, order, and purpose and more." Sandy contributed great information and we hope to hear from her in the future.*

From the above quotes one word stands out and was mentioned by most of these individuals and that is the word Constitution. We see many politicians today only reference the constitution when it suits their needs. Democrats say that it's an evolving document and can be changed at any time because we have problems in our country that need immediate correction. Republicans tell us the constitution is what we base our rights and should be followed and only changed when necessary. As a country there have been times in our history that the Constitution needed amendments to fix wrong that occurred at that time in history. We all came together and united to make those changes permanent. Another time was right after the Civil War regarding slavery. This country fixed a wrong and we moved on. The constitution is not an evolving document and should not be treated as such. Having those qualities to adhere to that historical document is great to look for in a candidate for political office.

When reading these quotes some people really thought hard about what they wanted to get across. We enjoyed when people started debating with each other which was the point we were trying to accomplish when we started this project. The more people we get thinking about politics, the better chances we have in educating each other. They also got spirited, and people got their points across. We all have our own opinions, that is what makes America great, and just because someone has a difference of opinion doesn't mean they should be treated differently.

Some countries evolved their constitution or just walked away from it, like Greece, Rome, Great, Britain, and Germany; these were once strong countries. By the way, this government, is ruining itself from the inside and it sure looks like we will be the next powerful country to fall—The United States of America. We have had the longest active constitution in the history of the world and we're entering a very scary phase that looks like the end may be coming, and we the great people of this country need to take the reins back from their government. We do that through voting.

*Mary: "Our government is completely corrupt with lobbyists and special interests' groups allowed to "buy" privilege. Congressmen and senators spend 90% of their day raising money for their next personal re-election campaign. They are not beholden to the people they represent, but to their biggest donors. This has happened over time and has nothing to do with the US Constitution and everything to do with corruption. The SYSTEM is corrupt! The individuals elected are complicit. The American people must demand a total overhaul starting with disallowing lobbyists to buy favors from their state rep's. America is actually being controlled by billionaires who manipulate government to benefit their agenda. All of the in-fighting today is created by false propaganda, a tool to keep the people confused and ignorant. It is a smoke screen for hiding truth — the truth of corruption. One of the worst of many is Rupert Murdoch."*

*Deborah: "Mary, Apparently you have no idea of just how much the Democrats are guilty of. I promise you that I have fact checked it and the Democrats have done many more evil things than you are aware of apparently. But I pray that God opens your eyes and so many others as well to just how corrupt the Democrats have been. It's all starting to come out now. Slowly but surely."*

*Mary: "Deborah let's just agree that both sides are responsible for 'dirty hands' politicking. No argument. However, the democrats offer policies that actually help people. I see nothing but resistance on the right. Trump himself is hopelessly corrupt and will be prosecuted. Why would I want to follow his parade? Why would anyone?"*

*Renee: "That they are not an election denier that they are not a Republican."*

*Jay: Dennis Gravelle, 1) What I'm looking for in a candidate is a strong commitment to progressive values: a commitment to democracy, challenging the plutocracy and income inequality, transfer of massive amounts of funding from the*

*Pentagon budget to fund a variety of human needs, support for the labor movement, support for public education, support for affordable housing, support for single-payer health care, support for expanded and affordable child care, an effective and reliable mass public transportation system, alternative energy development, pro-women's and gay rights, including pro-choice, among others.*

*2) As to whether Democrats and Republicans will ever work again, some of us think the Republican Party looks irretrievably broken and likely will split in coming years. That is, if what is now the Trumpist authoritarian personality cult doesn't seize power electorally or otherwise and draw the remnant non-Trump faction back in and decimate the opposition, including Democrats and virtually all else."*

When people reference the last administration to me it seems like they are not paying attention to their own party corruption. Every politician in my eyes is corrupt and are only looking to make themselves rich off the people. We can reference several resources that shows this current president is corrupt, along with all members of this congress. Here is an article I (Dennis) read violating laws they have created: 72 members of Congress have violated a law designed to prevent insider trading and stop conflicts-of-interest by Dave Levinthal Updated Oct 12, 2022

"Congress passed the law a decade ago to combat insider trading and conflicts of interest among their own members and force lawmakers to be more transparent about their personal financial dealings. A key provision of the law mandates that lawmakers publicly — and quickly — disclose any stock trade made by themselves, a spouse, or a dependent child."

-Senator Dianne Feinstein, a Democrat from California

"Feinstein was months late disclosing a five-figure investment her husband made into a private, youth-focused polling company."

-Senator Tommy Tuberville, a Republican from Alabama

Tuberville was weeks or months late in disclosing nearly 130 separate stock trades from January to May.

Read this article and it will show you that politicians from both parties violate their own laws and nothing happens to them. We always tell people to don't believe what we say, research what we talk about. The question is how much longer we the people going to put up with their corrupt nonsense. That is why we must vote. That is why we need constitutional candidates.

After finding the right candidate that has the qualities you want the next important part is to get out and vote for him or her. The sad part is that there are millions of registered voters who don't vote. There are several reasons for this and to name just a few. Conducting an online search about this topic I came across this article by the name of: "I don't plan to vote ever again: The psychology of why so many people don't vote, even in 2020" by Catherine Clifford. Published Fri, Oct 30, 2020, 9:01 AM EDT. Here are some excerpts from the article:

"I don't plan to vote ever again…and none of my family members are voting this year," says a thirty-six-year-old resident of Georgia, who says she is not a party-line voter and shared her thoughts with CNBC Make It, on condition of anonymity due to a fear of backlash. "We don't care who wins the election," because no elected politicians have helped during "these hard, dark times," she says.

"I don't feel represented by the candidates the parties in power keep offering up," says Norman, a self-described conservative millennial, writing for the online publication The Doe, which shares "anonymous narratives to promote civil discourse." "[A]nd I won't vote for a 'lesser evil,'" he says.

People are fed up with the political nonsense, so they refuse to vote for anyone. We must change that mentality and get people to think like the people I have mentioned above. Find the right candidate for you, and if you can't find one still vote and write your own name on the ballot, that should get politicians thinking that people don't believe in the system or them anymore.

We cannot be like that Georgia resident mentioned in the named article. We must vote to have our voices heard. That is why we must research candidates that best fit the mold. We need to elect politicians that don't represent party, they need to represent we the people.

Corruption and not being represented seems to be a strong combination. As you start getting back involved in your government and getting involved for the first time you'd ask yourself where this corruption starts at and we believe from the administrative state agencies of this government, which was started under President Franklin Delano Roosevelt (FDR). We will talk about corruption later in our book.

We will end this chapter with this final comment which we agree with.

***Christy:*** *"Vote like your life depends on it--because it does!!"*

We must stop voting for party and start voting for individuals. These parties have proven that they are not worthy of our time or votes. Read on, Patriots!!

# Chapter 4

# "THE FUTURE"

How do you feel about the future of this country?

The National debt for the United States is currently over $31 trillion dollars and climbing daily. Only once in our history our entire national debt was paid off. That was on January 8th, 1835, when Andrew Jackson was president. However, that was short lived because the government started given out surplus money to banks, and that led to the panic of 1837. During that time our government had to resume borrowing money again. The last time this country's national debt was under 10 trillion dollars was in 2007.

The Panic of 1837 was an economic downturn that left individuals unemployed and broke. The problems that caused this panic was banks giving out loans and printing large amounts of their money, kind of what our government is doing today by printing money which we don't have, which led to high inflation, like we have seen over the past two years with inflation running over 8 percent. President Jackson and the political leaders at that time caused money to depreciate, the same thing is happening today with our money. This pandemic lasted several years and due to these policies put forth by Jackson ended losing his next term for office. We have seen this problem before and it's only a matter of time before it happens again. Presidential administrations and politicians who instruct banks to give out loans to people who can't afford them which led to the housing collapse in 2008. Since 2019, we've had record unemployment and businesses were struggling to stay afloat. We have politicians that could care less about people and the struggle they endure to survive in our country today.

We look at the past to see what the future has in store for this country. When we don't learn from past mistakes, we are doomed to repeat them again. Every year our national debt soars past the year before. That shows us that politicians don't care or are so corrupt when spending our taxpayer money and each administration wants to spend money it doesn't have. Doesn't matter if you are a republican or democrat politicians. They all talk about slowing the national debt, but that's just what it is talk. It never gets accomplished.

These out-of-control taxes stated by the 16th amendment to the United States Constitution which modified article 1, section 9 which says everyone gets taxed the same. Congress has the power to lay and collect taxes on incomes from whatever source derived without apportionment among the several States and without regard to any census or enumeration was how this tax structure was pursued because the progressives knew the implementation of the administrative state that ballooned under FDR and has grown out of control since.

We believe that our country is on the decline and that our future is in serious trouble, thanks to these politicians. We believe that politicians are tyrants and need to be put in check. That's hard to accomplish when you have both major political parties spreading lies and misinformation saying everything is alright, which in fact is not the case. We the people feel our future doesn't look bright, thanks to this government. The amount of income taxes we pay is out of control. We are getting taxed for everything we do in this country. From state tax, county tax, local taxes, vehicle tax, house taxes, school taxes, even when we go out to eat, we must pay a sales tax. It never ends, and it seems like the government wants to find more ways to make us pay more, we can't afford it anymore. More and more people feel that the future looks depressing to them, especially with the rising cost of health care and buying a house has most of America unable to live the American dream.

People feel that the rights we had as kids, the rights under the Declaration of Independence which states: "We hold these truths to be self-evident, that all men are created equal, that they are endowed by their Creator with certain unalienable Rights, that among these are Life, Liberty and the pursuit of Happiness.—That to secure these rights, Governments are instituted among Men, deriving their just powers from the consent of the governed, —That whenever any Form of Government becomes destructive of these ends, it is the Right of the People to alter or to abolish it, and to institute new Government, laying its foundation on such principles and organizing its powers in such form, as to them shall seem most likely to affect their Safety and Happiness. Prudence, indeed, will dictate that Governments long established should not be changed for light and transient causes; and accordingly, all experience hath shewn, that mankind is more disposed to suffer, while evils are sufferable, than to right themselves by abolishing the forms to which they are accustomed."

People also feel their rights are being taken away daily, and that our children and future generations will not have the same liberties as we did as children, we cannot let that happen. According to the Declaration of Independence those rights come from God and our politicians have lost sight of that. We must stop believing these politicians of today are the answer we need. People are worried about the United States and several individuals believe we're heading down the wrong road. Unfortunately, there's another passage that people seem to have forgotten or just have not learned, this one comes from the preamble of the Constitution which states blessings of liberty to us and our posterity. Posterity will be a forgotten word in future generations. Not only in the future, but citizens of today are also losing their posterity. Read on to see what they said.

*Lois:* *"I see a country confused, WEIRD, and sad, right now...I see kids not being kids, but sexual objects. I see pedophilia (especially in the democratic party) becoming "normal"...I see people eating fake food instead of meat, fruit, and vegetables... I see paper money and coins gone; you will get a chip in your body to "pay" for things... I see the human race slowly fade out, only a select few will survive, AI will be in every job, for the wealthy (only), slavery will make a strong comeback, and education will not be for the poor, the poor will be programmed to serve the rich (sound familiar?) ... I see a Godless world, and many people will feel the rath, like it says in the bible, you will burn.... But honestly, has the world ever been kind? Helpful? Loving? World leaders have ruined mankind since the Romans...Satan will always roam the earth, just like bastard politicians and wealthy people who have bad intentions...."*

*James:* *"The nation is now in the hands of the wealthy. Rather it is individuals or corporations. They only care about making more and more. And give as little as possible back to the workers. As it has been planned for a century plus. As far as the so-called Nation. They will sustain it as long as there are profits to be made. Only an outside force will end this as it has always been with any great nation or civilization. Rather it is a force from space, internal earth or mankind destroying themselves. Beware of any entity that comes as the answer to all problems and shows greatness that wins the minds and hearts of the multitudes. People rely on Kings and Hero's too much."*

**Diane:** *"How can anyone see what's happened since Biden took office and NOT see where we are headed?? He is driving us to the brink…. allowing millions to cross our Southern border …God only knows what they are letting through. I have no problem with people wanting a better life…. but do it LEGALLY!!! And be willing to work for the life you want…. not expect it to be handed to you!! They come here with nothing…. we give them cell phones, clothes, housing, medical care, food….and then have to educate their kids in already overcrowded schools with special exemptions because they don't speak English. There is no other country STUPID enough to just allow anyone and everybody to come into their country. Lots of criminals have come through…. several on the "do not fly" list, and we don't even know where they are!! Many want to do us harm….and yet the "Dims" see none of this as problematic…. unless of course, these people end up on THEIR doorstep. We are definitely heading for a recession, Bill Gates and China buying up tons of farmland, much of it near our military bases….am I the ONLY ONE who sees a problem with this???"*

**Montee:** *"If you want my honest opinion, the future of the United States is bleak. I honestly believe it is time for Texas to once again take its place among the Nations"*

**Lola Tungl:** *"What's going on has complicated causes with roots that go way back at least as far as Reagan. Add COVID and Trump and we now have political BS that is divisive and dangerous. It doesn't look good for the future. There are no quick fixes no matter which party is in control."*

**Jeannie:** *"This is not America anymore. We are nothing more than a soup pot."*

**Elizabeth:** *"Dennis Gravelle, I agree sadly the lesser of two evils is our last bastion of hope right now of we can stop the republican party from taking us down the Hitler path, then we can start to deconstruct the system unlike the Republicans at least the Dems know reality is not based on emotion but facts and with the election of more progressive candidates we can begin to make the changes. As I told my oldest son one day you can eat a bear, but you can't eat it all at once. We have to start somewhere the first step beating the fascist party and destroying them. The more progressives the better. I never understood what people fear about progress. Everything changes and these changes are what we must so to become the truly Free society that we have always claimed to be."*

**Mike:** *"MO, the future of this country will depend on the worth of the US dollars. Henry Ford said something to the effect of "if the people knew how their dollar actually works, they would revolt tomorrow."*

***Charlotte:*** *"Scary, worry about my grandchildren, what will their life be like. The people now that are in office are it trustworthy. I do not trust them at all."*

***Jeff:*** *"It's hard to be positive when the country is being intentionally destroyed."*

***Eman:*** *"People now have less respect less care for human life less care for helping one another. Too many sensitive people too many people with lack of common sense not enough proper education for our children. Parents aren't disciplining their kids' parents aren't parenting anymore instead throwing a tablet or phone in front of them to keep them entertained. Not enough outdoor activities going on anymore instead they're on electronic devices. Kids are getting confused by crazy media and calling themselves transgender and other things of that nature. Too much porn too much drugs. Men aren't men these days instead they're feminized version. Too much pot smoking not enough God-fearing people. People are becoming soft and dumb and without thought of their own. Corrupt fraudulent politicians running around taking our freedoms little by little. It's not a good time to raise kids due to all the awful things being taught in school and the influences of the media.... it's an awful time. If you ignore it and be real, it's not so bad but you'll be playing tug of war with your kids and society influencing them... It's a nonstop battle to be normal. Normal now is frowned upon...yeah man shit is crazy but probably too late to fix..."*

*"Dennis Gravelle, that's the problem. No one is uniting. People are bitter and selfish. Just the other day my son, daughter and I were flying a small foam plane around our neighborhood, when it went out if range and landed in someone yard in the next street. We asked the owner which was outside if we could look back in her yard to see if it's there and get it...she said no her gates are locked. I politely asked if she could please open them because there is a good chance the plane is there. She said she was too busy with an attitude. Granted I'm with my little children otherwise I would of let her have it. I asked if I could just hop the fence and wouldn't be any bother to her. She said no. I noticed an older woman next door and asked her if I could go in her yard she said absolutely, and I peeked over from there to the other yard m saw the plain. older woman obviously didn't care for her neighbor either, but she did tell her it's there. Finally with a huge attitude she got it and roughly gave it to me...my little son asked me why she was so mad... This is the kind of people we have in this country now..."*

***Ray:*** *"It looks like we are in trouble for sure, but the Constitution is still strong and when it is challenged, it wins. We need to do all that we can through government and politics, but our hope is in the Lord.*

*It looks like we are in trouble for sure, but the Constitution is still strong and when it is challenged, it wins. We need to do all that we can through government and politics, but our hope is in the Lord. Psalm 33:12.* "

**Ray:** *"Lonnie, Democrats are the best example of what is wrong with America today. My parents were dems at one time but came out from that wicked foolishness. Dems are against everything that is honored in Scripture and for everything that is perverted. You cannot pray one way and vote another . That does not make any sense. Isaiah 5:20 speaks to that."*

We believe that most people in this country have lost faith in God. If we don't believe God touched this country, that shows we have lost faith in the Almighty. Many people look out at what is going on with this country and don't understand why their God is making every one of us feel like we are going through hell. What have we done to deserve this kind of hatred and selfishness with so many people today? It's as if the citizens of this country have gone crazy. Children can't even go outside to play with friends anymore, parents think they are going to be shot. That's not everywhere, we have some places where kids can and do spend their days outside. In our big cities crime is out of control thanks to politicians. So, people of course have lost faith in God.

Psalm 33:12 states "Blessed is the Nation whose God is the Lord; and the people he hath chosen for his own inheritance. We all need to have faith that God will do what he has promised, even when things are tough. Isiah 5:20 says "move on to them that call evil good, and good evil, that put darkness for light, and light for darkness, that put bitter for sweet and sweet for bitter. This is exactly what is happening with politics today. We must wake up to this new reality that one day we might lose all our freedoms, the American dream will be gone, and bread lines will occur once more. That is how serious of a problem we have in America today.

**Daniel:** *"Dennis the two-party system has nothing to do with it. It's actually the people, today people don't care about others a few want to tell us how to live and what we should do. Look what happened on Martha's Vineyard those rich people talk about sanctuary, and all are welcome, well we all witnessed that wasn't true they kicked the illegals off their island in less than 40 hours. Right now, the future is grim, but* *hopefully after November 8, we will have a new speaker and a new senate leader and stop Biden from digging us into a deeper hole. I'm a Democrat and I'm voting red this year; we need the balance. I am concerned of what is or could happen to my children and grandchildren. Look at how poor our education system has gotten with this leadership. Need I say anymore?"*

**Bryon:** *"I believe that our 2-party system is a disaster. Representative government was never meant to be entitled representatives making themselves and their families rich on the people's taxes. It is two trains, one on the left track, one on the right track, headed off the same cliff."*

**Anonymous:** *"Dennis Gravelle, Democrats right now at least are helping the country as well as a few Republicans, but what have Republicans brought to the table since Obama was elected? They vote no on everything outside of tax cuts and help to those that need it and destroying healthcare. Now we have Trumpers who's only agenda is power, how to get it how to retain it. We need term limits a test to show you have at least knowledge of the 3 branches of government and how it works. The country is going to die from too far left to far right and allowing those with the IQ of a houseplant to govern us"*

**Clay:** *"Well as long as we allow the Left to Cheat on Elections. Install Idiots to lead this great nation. Get caught up in the Clean Energy BS. Let the Major networks keep spreading disinformation and not reporting the truth. I fear for the world my Grandkids will be dealing with. Allow the country to be walked on by the Chinese and Allow people to flood across the border unchecked. At some point the madness needs to stop."*

**Anonymous**: *"It depends on who gets to lead the country, you get DeSantis in office, and it will be 4 years of trying to kill democracy and putting in place people rules and laws to keep the lunatics running the country for decades. We can't survive when you have Greene's Boeberts in office and then have them shove a moron like Dr. Oz on us and the blithering idiot Walker, not to mention the old geezers in office. My family is different collection of races, that's what scares me the most, trump kicked over the rocks and gave those pieces of shit racists a voice, returning them to under their rocks will take decades and longer if republicans keep power. They'd love nothing better than to go back in time to a place that never existed (Mayberry was a tv town) then strip us of social security and Medicare or privatization of both to make Wall Street rich."*

***Ruben:*** *"The current state of most of the people in the United States who are full of hatred for believing a person that is a pathological liar who is dividing Americans, just for his own gain, how can a person with a minimum of intelligence with all the real evidence follows his believing. I feel very sorry for my country.*　"

***Scott:*** *"Dennis Gravelle, Only the democrat party fixes actual Presidential elections. I already knew like everyone else, that when an election is close, democrats will cheat to win it. History proves this. "Vote early and vote often" is the motto in Cook County.*

***Harry S:*** *"Our problem is that the two parties in control are just the left and right wings of the Socialist Party. Their fixation on Keynesian economics is driving us toward a cliff."*

Read up on Keynesian economics: it's interesting. At this time, we want to tell our theory of these two parties called the left and right wings. The left wing we have democrats like Bernie Sanders, Alexandria Ocasio Cortez (AOC) who are people who have admitted they want government control. And then you have the right side, like Marjorie Taylor Greene and Laruen Bobbitt who are extremists. So, it's both parties that have elected politicians that are more passionate than most of them. Most Americans are moderate, center-minded people, and individuals like the ones mentioned get their blood boiling.

We call it the pendulum swing and notice that when the pendulum swings, we see that it only goes left and right. It does not move forward or backward. Good thing it doesn't go backward, or this country would be in a lot of trouble. We always have change on the pendulum—every two years in Washington, when we vote in federal elections, and once every four years for President. It's called Pendulum Democracy and it's a model democracy in which both political parties fight for control of this pendulum.

Our so-called leaders want their names highlighted in a capital letters in the biggest font possible. They want to make it known they are in charge, and that we the people are the voter/spectators as an audience democracy. Since the pendulum only swings left and right, there is no moving forward. So, we the constituents will always come up with the short end of the pendulum. Woodrow Wilson said in a speech. "The only difference between socialist and progressivism is that socialists want change through revolt, progressives want change through the administrative state."

These politicians know we have a sensitive electorate, and they will do whatever they can to keep you on one side. Through misinformation and segregation, we have a divided USA. The left side, the liberal pendulum is long and slow. Politicians try to take away our constitutional rights a little at a time, so you barely notice it. Remember, these elected officials have become tyrannical and will do what they need to do to keep the people scared and out of their way. It's a 'winner take all' outcome, and everyone wants to be a winner, right? Politicians understand this and will lie to our faces to tell us their policies are better than the other's side. One party, one ideology. That's what they want you to believe. We need to remember what type of government we have here in America. It's a representative, Republic type of government with three separate branches of government with three separate responsibilities with the constitution as the law of the land.

U.S. elections keeps shifting the pendulum left and right and people are getting more confused. Where democrat presidents try to regulate, republican presidents try to deregulate, and each party tries to reverse policies instead of working to strengthen them. The pendulum will never move forward with two parties with left to right swinging in control of government.

We always mention the political corruption that Washington politicians get away with day after day, and if a non-elected individual is corrupt, they get put through hell, and they should, and so should politicians. Politicians should not get a free ride; it just puts them on a power trip.

At this time in our history the pendulum is in the PITS. The back and forth between these two parties will continue to cause havoc on American citizens unless we the people say we're not going to take it anymore. We must be the ones that send a message to these two major parties that we the people are fed up with their politics, or we will never move forward. If we are not moving forward, we only slide left and right, so we can never get ahead so we all win, not politicians but every United States citizen. We must stop the political pendulum. Secure voting rights for every registered voter, that's how we put the people back in control of this government, leaving political parties out altogether. We all know that our current politicians who can stop this pendulum won't do it, they are sucked in the vacuum too far. We the people must fight for democracy before these politicians take it all away and we have lost all our freedoms.

***John:*** *"If we do not get back to/follow the constraints of our Constitutional Republic we will be on the junk-heap of history's many failed command economies... wish it wasn't so"*

***Madeleine:*** *"With this push to Globalization the future is very much taken out of nations hands. People get post in Globalization that's why it has to be resisted. If you give up things will only get worse be proud stand up and don t leave it to others. Just do your bit and the future will still be your and not taken away from you by others"*

***Chris:*** *"How do I see the future for myself, children, and grandchildren? As a man that's simple. Depends on how much work I want to do for them. Protecting them, teaching them, and so on. I know for me and my family we are going to be great. I live by the three Gs. God, Guns, and Glory! So yes, I would think the future for at least my family will always be good. As a country, are we in trouble thanks to our current two-party system? I think that's the least of the problems. Our constitutional rights are all that matter to me. If our "government" fails. I know how to live, and life will move forward. We might not have money anymore, but I know how to haggle and barter very well. We might get to know our neighbors again, but I'm ok with that. Leave the matrix and just live!"*

***Deirdre:*** *"We are all responsible for our future. We create and make change by standing up to the people around us, including government when wrongs are committed on society. Change does not happen; things do not improve if we sit back and just chat about issues but don't actively do something about it and allow what is wrong to continue. That is why there are protests, that is why there are community groups, that is why we often see a single person stand up, but it really helps if others backup these people. We cannot expect others to carry the burden and create change for us. We are all responsible. Some don't like to become involved in protests and that's okay as there are other ways to affect change. We are all in this mess because we allowed it. Victim mentality does not create change, we all need to create change. Too many of us have sat back for too long and chatted about issues but not become actively involved in creating a better world. We have allowed our governments to behave the way they do, and we are responsible. We often wish and expect others to magically create the changes we would like but the reality is it's up to all of us. No one will save us but us. We all need to be creating the change for ourselves and our children. Next time something happens that affects society, affects us all, seek out ways to change it. Dwelling* *in negativity does not help as that just pulls everyone down. Rather lift to the positive and actively find and promote ways to improve all our lives. Waiting for tomorrow for someone to change something while it progressively gets worse will not create change. We live in the present and we all need to be the change we want to see now in this moment, today. Be the change you want to see.* ♡ *We love the optimism of several comments we received from these  individuals. We should all be more positive like they are. We have the power in our hands to take this country back anytime we want, we just must unite to do just that. This last quote sums up this chapter very well.*

**Gigi:** *"The future is subject to change."*

No one can argue with that.

# Chapter 5

# "Media Outlets"

Why do you trust the media, or don't you trust the media?

Why are medias outlets so biased towards republicans and democrats?

We don't think most people really get it about Mainstream media. There used to be a time when commentators were respected, and they did a great job. What they did was report the news, good and bad, and that's what people wanted to hear. Today is so different, we have reached a point in our history where media outlets are a joke, but not laughable. They are downright awful, and they believe that listeners are loyal subjects and that it's their job to make those listeners believe anything they say. We call it brainwashing.

What is Political Journalism? Well, its goal is to provide voters with the information to formulate their own opinion and participate in community, local or national matters that will affect them. That is what these news stations should be doing, but what do they do today, is give us their opinions and always try to put a different spin on the story. So, even if they have all the facts, they will withhold information to create panic in listeners. Every news organization does this; they only tell us what they want us to hear, not the truth.

The truth does not sell stories, misinformation does that. People love to hear gossip about anything and everything, so why should the news media be any different? Listen to FOX news to get their spin on politics, then CNN to get their spin on it and then you can find where the truth lies. We must understand that they are both withholding information and just stating talking points for politicians; that is for both parties. It's sad that media outlets and commentators have become this way. This is just an opinion, but it certainly seems like the news is reporting more like social media than investigative reporting. They used to work hand in hand with the written press, now they both work like social media, no facts needed, just shock and awe to make a short story. It seems like they don't spend more than a handful of seconds on any topic.

What can we do about it? How do we hold the media accountable when we can't even hold our politicians accountable? There are a few different ways to take them to task. A few examples are just turning off news outlets altogether. When they start losing thousands of listeners maybe the dim light will get a new bulb. Stop buying newspapers like the NY Times, NY Post, and National Review, the Wall Street Journal, the American Conservative, and any local newspapers that you can buy, just stop supporting them. Try and find an independent channel to listen to—we haven't found any yet, but we're still looking. We get our political news, not just from one source, but several.

Don't buy into the hype. Don't get brainwashed by these stations. There are already enough brainwashed individuals in this country. Stay away from those new hosts that have conspiracy theories. We have enough of them out there, from left-wing to right-wing groups that also want to destroy America.

Thirty-six percent of individuals living in the country have a "great deal" or "fair amount" of trust in mass media, which means over 60% of the population does not trust them. Democrats trust the media the most at 68%, Independent trust is at 31% and Republican trust stands at 11%.

We always hear the word transparency today, but do we get that? In our opinion, no. We don't get it from our presidential administration, we sure as heck don't get it from members of Congress, and nothing along the line of transparency with our media outlets and commentators. They need to earn our trust back and we must hold them accountable when they don't tell the entire story. They always leave out words and sentences from politicians who oppose their network.

We have enough corruption in politics, and I found this next information from PEW research:

"Americans blame unfair news coverage on media outlets, not the journalists who work for them in October 2020. Overall, about eight in ten Americans (79%) say news organizations tend to favor one side when presenting the news on political and social issues, according to a survey conducted Feb. 18 to March 2, 2020. Far fewer (20%) say these organizations deal fairly with all sides."

In 1995 Peter Vanderwicken wrote *Why the News is not the Truth* and I'm sure it is more prevalent today:

"The U.S. press, like the U.S. government, is a corrupt and troubled institution. Corrupt not so much in the sense that it accepts bribes but in a systemic sense. It fails to do what it claims to do, what it should do, and what society expects it to do.

"The news media and the government are entwined in a vicious circle of mutual manipulation, mythmaking, and self-interest. Journalists need crises to dramatize news, and government officials need to appear to be responding to crises. Too often, the crises are not really crises but joint fabrications. The two institutions have become so ensnared in a symbiotic web of lies that the news media are unable to tell the public what is true, and the government is unable to govern effectively."

Do your homework; the media as well as our current government clowns are worthless and tyrants and thieves, and that is our opinion. Neither tell the truth and we the people don't hold them accountable.

*Anonymous:* "A *fantastic question. For me as an Australian, it all started in 2015 when the election of the century was looming. Donald Trump vs Hillary Clinton. I knew there were two main parties in the US Democrats and Republicans, and to be perfectly honest I really didn't know that much or really care who won. Personally, I had Barrack Obama's back when he got in. As time went on with Obama, not was all as it seemed...I noticed great unrest in the world with him present, and nothing really changed. Some things got worse...notably Isis and US race relations. Very disheartening- considering I liked him, and he appeared very smooth. Then when Hillary ran against Trump I saw deeper. It was as though the whole mainstream media was behind this massive smear campaign. Russian collusion and all kinds of ridiculous attacks on the Don... Very mean-spirited stuff. It got downright weird and nasty. I started to notice Obama had a very condescending and vicious side to him. Hillary too. When Trump won, the democrat reaction was very telling. I immediately knew I was right to back Trump. He was up to his neck in democrat lies. It got worse. Then came the race riots, which the democrats and media romanticized. Suddenly, every republican was a racist. It occurred to me I may have missed something about American culture...but here it was. And it was ugly. So, after 6 years of left wing hate and vitriol, I now know who owns the media...the fact checks...the politicians themselves. The U.N. Undoubtedly the worst collection of human scum on the face of the earth. Donald Trump the maverick made the swamp monsters surface, and I will never forget. They live on both sides of politics, but I assure you that net zero is the fastest way to globalist hell."*

**Bobbie:** *"I don't trust the media as they don't report actual facts. They report a narrative they want people to believe. They are paid for by the people who want this narrative put out there It's just about impossible to find any news outlet that isn't biased one way or another.*

*I used to be one of these people that followed the news and believe, for the most part, what was being reported. However, as time went on and as I grew older, I started to notice more - like how the different outlets, all reporting on the same story, report contrary things. As social media become more and more a part of everyone's lives, I noticed how a political person would say something and the media would twist it to say what fit their narrative. I no longer follow the news. I will check it every so often to find out about weather, traffic, basic stuff but turn it off when it starts pushing the narrative Whatever happened to journalistic integrity?"*

**James:** *"You have to double check from any sources any news that you get from anybody. Yes, media is biased based on who owns the particular franchise or the company that owns the media outlet. As they say follow the money. But it's not just a Democrat and Republican thing it's more so the owner of the station and who that person favors. But then again, we did see Bernie Sanders purposely get snubbed by the media in favor of Hillary even by so-called liberal outlets. And throughout our history media has somewhat been controlled by the government especially propaganda against countries that we don't like. And of course, the government has kept tabs on various news outlets and such to control the outlet and the information that is given to the public. We all think we're free and have freedom of choice and realize very little that we all are controlled not only through economics but through the information we are fed by whoever it is that has the biggest money. But through my '63 years and my younger years the only true source of information and news that was honest and you could rely on was ham radio operators in various countries that would talk to each other. So, all in all I think it is the wealthy that control what information you get no matter what source you get it from. And unless we can go back to the days of large ham radio usage nobody will really know the truth or what's truly going on. Just my input just my opinion. I use Google voice and it changes my word so excuse the editing as I go along after the fact."*

**Lori:** *"Because they lie? On two occasions when I was at protests/marches in Boston the media posted a pic of the first with a scattering of people (not only was the* *true march upwards of 500 but they took and posted pictures of the wrong group of people) and the second the media said there were a few dozen. We had a drone which counted 2 THOUSAND"*

***Jane:*** *"Because hatred and prejudice are PROFITABLE"*

***Hakon:*** *"I don't trust the MSM. They have been proven, on fat too many occasions to be pushing false narratives. That goes for both sides. The lies are so prevalent in media today it's impossible to know who is telling the truth. Left: "such n such city saw mostly peaceful protests today..." The Right on the same story: "people are rioting in the streets and burning down homes and businesses." This is just one example in a long history of contradictory stories run by MSM over the past 20 years."*

***Pamela:*** *"Dennis Gravelle, they are nothing but paid pre-programmed liars."*

***Ryan:*** *"People get involved in media because THEY really want to be heard, not because they want to report what other people are saying and doing. They feel so hard about things, and they want others' hearts to bleed the same as theirs, so they (usually liberals) are attracted to an occupation that gives them a pulpit. Liberal ideas defy common sense, so only by repetition and gas-lighting of the public through the media can they hope to gain traction."*

***Charlotte:*** *"I totally do not trust the media. Anyone who does is doing drugs. 2nd? Because they only listen to democrats. But I feel that some are starting to realize the inflation deal and many other things are not working for the country. God help us."*

***Mary:*** *"Dennis the media has turned to yellow journalism. I have found none of them seem to post what is truly said"*

We are glad that Mary brought up yellow journalism. That is exactly what these organizations are doing to sell their news stations. They list one minor fact and then they hype up the rest of the story, designed to confuse or arouse you. News does not sell facts, they sell sensationalism. Yellow journalism "refers to **sensationalistic or biased stories that newspapers present as objective truth**. Established late 19th-century journalists coined the term to belittle the unconventional techniques of their rivals." Today, it is used best by social media platforms, such as Twitter, Facebook, and I'm sure we can list many more. "Television and the Internet make good use of yellow journalism by running sensationalized headlines typed in big, vivid fonts, consisting of news that is less than well-researched."

**Kory:** *"News is a for profit business, on TV, social media etc. If it's for profit, it's beholden to the shareholder, not the truth. Fox News learned early on, if they can cater to, and confirm the biases and fears, of a certain percentage of the population, they can line their pockets with gold. And if they keep stoking fear in those folks, they will keep watching. And after 20 years of this, the other side decided to jump in and now it's a 2-sided war instead of just a one-sided propaganda machine."*

**Carrie:** *"All media is "influence". Influenced minds make poor decisions (and not of their own). The same as law is simply an opinion and the majority rules."*

**Michele:** *"I don't trust the media to cover politics evenly and without bias. When they make excuses for Joe Biden or Fetterman for their words and actions yet if a Republican were to have the same issues, they would be slammed and condemned. When the story doesn't meet their narratives, they just don't cover it at all. When facts come out that defeat their narrative, they will not correct themselves publicly. They issue a small retraction online which no one will see."*

**Karen:** *"I just an e-mail from an independent press and they said that Corporate Media is not broken, it is designed to serve corporate power. Then they gave me a list of who funds the things we see. It is giant corporations and banks."*

**Christopher:** *Dennis Gravelle, thank you for asking. I'm afraid my answer would be too far extreme that you probably wouldn't want to include it, and I'm trying to stay out of fb jail. For my business pages, so I'll keep it short and sweet. The system that peoples believe exists, doesn't. What's actually happening behind them closed doors and elitist meetings, we'll never know until it's too late, and even then, we'll never truly know the full extent of the severity we face on a regular. The media? Is paid and bought, like most of the rest of the "system"... It's dogma and doctrine. I've spent nearly 2 decades warning about this, to never trust gov or the media, most of science and education as well. The truth exists, if you don't get lost looking for it, designed that way since 4000 years ago!"*

**Murl:** *"I do not trust most media outlets. This is because they have basically become propaganda machines for the Democratic Party and progressive ideology."*

**Carol:** *"I Don't like the media. Why doesn't fact check do them for the untrue remarks made."*

**Jim:** *"First of all, you need to define "media". It used to mean newspapers, magazines, TV, and radio. Now it not only encompasses those, but you can add internet blogs, chats, cable TV, and dark internet sites that only those with a technical or* *ideological bias seem to access. An analogous meaning would be much like a library, in terms of variation of knowledge, and bias. Libraries contain books, magazines, newspapers that expound their particular view of anything from science to ideologies (both political and religious), but to label a "library" as something that you either trust, or do not trust, is the same as asking whether or not you trust the "media". Just what "media" is the question targeting? There is a huge media universe whose financial existence depends upon how many "eyeballs" or ears, are looking at that particular site, network, blog, or radio program. So, "trust" in the media is a tremendous reach of a very wide paint brush. The biases of each segment of the "media", in America, depends solely upon the number of eyeballs, or ears that will keep those particular members of the medial in financial health. To me, those who are in agreement with those particular segments in "the media", are more likely to spend time watching and listening to those particular segments (either democratic, or republican). When a certain segment of the medial describes, and keeps preaching what you believe, you are a captured audience, and that particular segment can use your collective "eyeballs" to enhance themselves with advertising that is dependent upon the number of "eyeballs" that are present."*

*__Terry:__ "I don't trust the media! Liberals hate Republicans, we are for Law and order."*

*__Julie:__ "There are very few honest journalists & these would never reach mainstream. Most are actors, reading a script & pushing an agenda. RIP true journalism."*

*There is an old statement that has become irrelevant in today's news and that's called group thought which means no good for the news industry. Where have all the good journalists gone like Paul Harvey and Walter Cronkite who didn't have an opinion one way or another about the story or the outcome. They just reported the news. Journalists these days could you a great lesson on integrity. Our media is starting to be labeled as Federal-Run media outlets, like China, Russia, and Iran, who all run their state media and the narrative, since they take their direction from the tyrants in Washington D.C. At one time, our country had investigative journalism and tough questions were asked by reporters. These soft questions they ask candidates it laughable. We need reporters that will investigate this government and let the people know what is going on within our federal agencies.*

*__Lola:__ "Trump adds a different aspect to this argument. He has managed to convince a lot of people that truth are lies. Every he's caught doing is fake news. Qanon flourishes, the big lie of election fraud is spread by members of his party, the Trumplicans, while members of the true Republican party are silent afraid to buck the* *tide. There are many news agencies that report the same things. Then there is Fox. I get my news from a lot of places and generally believe that it is truthful. Fox talking heads are entertainment.*

**Kevin:** *"It sounds like you get your news from CNN and MSNBC. Who are both socialist propaganda outlets. If you truly think creepy Joe got more votes, then any other President in our history. Then you are the problem. The media is controlled by the same people who want a one world government to usher in the Antichrist."*

We always enjoy reading comments, where so many people took the time to respond to our questions. We even liked it more when those people started to talk to each other about each topic. It's funny to me that individuals only believe that President Trump was the biggest liar on the face of the earth. We are not saying he didn't lie. We just find it amazing, and people don't think the Democrats and President Biden have lied during the past two years. Every politician lies. As they first sit down in the halls of Congress, I imagine one of the first classes is "How do we screw the American people?" They do that with their lies and deception.

**Mark:** *"The question you ask goes beyond American shores, it's global, since around 1992 our media have been charged with presenting political "Agendas and Narratives and what is called Safe Messages" that fly in the face of Freedom and Truth, all orchestrated by Agenda 21/30 which is a very real threat to the free world. And now we find ourselves polarized by these policies, there are those that haven't raised their heads and contemplated "something is very wrong" and then there is an ever-increasing number that now see how our lives and the very future of humanity is being steered nefariously to a dystopian future that is unwelcome and unwanted. The lie is so big and immersive that it's hard for many to see. – Regards, Mark."*

**Paul:** *"The media in every mainstream form is biased towards an agenda set out by corporate elites to get the world running the way they want it, look at Ukraine, covid etc., it is totally corrupt and all mainstream media needs taken out and totally organized differently to tell the news completely*

**Anonymous:** *"The media is owned by the elite. Follow the money. Those people dictate what can and can't be said. Even had a friend that works with mainstream media that admits this. They are designed to keep Americans separated. As long as we fight one another, we are not pushing them out of office."*

***Jeremy:*** *"There is only one, singular ruling class in America. They own both parties and all mainstream media outlets. Any division is controlled opposition. Any friction between the parties are by design to divide the peons. They focus on divisive issues intentionally. They magnify with their controlled mouthpieces in government and television. Good politicians are few and far between and will never gain traction without control of the narrative."*

***Gail:*** *"I do not believe that the USA will exist by the end of this decade. I'm just finishing up a book I'm writing about how we went off the rails in the coup d'état of March 6, 1819. That's when the Supreme Court decreed that our constitution is unconstitutional. It then replaced our constitutional republic with a national common law government, with the court as its self-appointed Caesar sharing a throne. The constitutional government could have worked, but the wealthy were unwilling to accept equality and freedom. They wanted POWER and money. I doubt my 25-year-old granddaughter will survive to die of a natural death." "I would support a constitutional amendment banning all political parties and any funding of them by more than $1.00 per voter per candidate in their district."*

***Randy:*** *"Ok by me. The media is always going to be bias. We as citizens have to understand this and dig for the real truth. Like people who thought smoking was cool back when we were young. Everyone who knew they were harmful. There were still those who lied to themselves to follow the crowd."*

***Jason:*** *"All media is corrupt. Networks/print/websites rely on advertising to drive revenue, and advertisers want viewers. They must do something to stand out as the preferred source of information. I believe we can all agree on this. I believe most of us can also agree that corporations have a primary interest in maximizing shareholder values. When we consider the vast choices, consumers have to choose from, obviously the competition requires an organization to elevate themselves above the other options. Sensationalism is the easiest way to draw in the needed consumers. Sensationalism eventually became commonplace, so a need to include opinions was created. The differences in opinions very quickly led to polarization. I don't trust the media because being trustworthy is not a priority for them anymore. Truth and opinion do not usually coexist. Where I differ from most of the others in this group is the fact, I don't support either Democrats or Republicans. I see the corruption on both sides. Most people look past the issues and vote based on party rather than issues (although most career politicians claim to align with the values of their voters). The result is that media sources must choose who to target. This leads to very pro-Republican and conversely* *pro-Democrat media. Politicians do it for money and power. Media does it for money and fame. At no point does a politician or a media organization do anything for me, they only exist to serve their own interests. I doubt I provided any new information, but you asked."*

When I first met Jack Young and we started doing our podcast called, "Meet at the Tavern," now called Stand United with Jack and Dennis one of the first comments he made was this: "My mother always told me when I was a child to get away from that idiot box called the television." That is what we feel Mainstream news media and social media outlets are today. The idiots on television, Facebook, and Twitter. If you want the real news, get out of your house, and talk to your neighbors, join different groups such as the Moose Lodge or the American Legion. There are many organizations out there, for you to become involved. Talking with these folks will tell you exactly what is happening in your community. You will talk to others that feel just like you do. You don't need to listen to biased news media anymore. If you can't get out of the house, go to Google research and other search engines that will help you get the answers you need. When you find a subject that interests you, research more than one article, each source will give you more information and then you make the determination on where to find common ground. We will talk about how we move forward with our country at the end of this book and what we feel needs to be accomplished when Americans stand united. This last comment we believe sums it up for the rest of us.

**Tania:** *"The media is trying to destroy this country. They feed hate. How long can a divided house stand?"*

Right now, what we have in Washington, D.C. politics is a house divided, and a nation cannot stand when that happens. Thanks to politicians of the democratic and republican parties and news media, the house is about ready to collapse unless we the people do something. There are several reasons why we are a divided nation. Read on to hear more from the people!!

# Chapter 6

# "White Supremacy"

Do you believe that there is white supremacy in our society, or do you think all races and genders can work and live together in their respected communities and be friends?

Expand on your answers as to why or why not you believe in white supremacy or why you don't believe in it?

White supremacy is a belief that white people are a superior race with the right to dominate society at the expense of other racial and ethnic groups. White supremacy has morphed into a political ideology that affects socioeconomic and legal structures within the United States.

This will be a short chapter for all to read. We don't want to spend a lot of time on it, because it spreads hate on hate, and that is not what this country is about. We are about building a better future for us and our families. We are coming up on the year 2023 and there is no place for hate or racism in this society. Do we believe we have racists in our society? Yes, we do, however it isn't just white people that are racist towards the black community, we also have individuals in the black community, that are racist towards white people. Please ask yourself this question of why politicians were so afraid of Dr. Martin Luther King. The answer is he was on the cusp of bringing this country together and people of all races were starting to unite.

Where the white conspiracy started was with our elected politicians. They created this false narrative which they tried to use as a political wedge to put between races and religions. They have been trying to segregate we the people by race for as long as we remember. At this time in our history, they are very close to accomplishing that, we cannot let that happen. Here is a quote from President Biden regarding this issue, "White supremacists will not have the last word and this venom and violence cannot be the story of our time."

"White supremacy and all forms of hate-fueled violence have no place in America. Failure to call it out is complicity. Silence is complicity. And we cannot remain silent."

We can agree with that statement, we don't have a place in America for hate. In 2020, during his Presidential campaign, Biden did speak out against violence in the streets across our cities. He had to remain neutral and not campaign too hard on it, because most of his democratic leaders wanted to defund the police. Now, that he is in office, with the majority of both houses, he had the opportunity to ensure more police officers were on the streets. They passed major legislation with pork including funds for politicians, but no legislation on putting more cops on the beat.

It has been proven that the democratic party has been a racist party forever. Remember Senator Byrd from West Virginia, he was the president for the clan back in the day. In 1981, Biden opposed busing to desegregate schools. Even his Vice-President criticized him during their campaign debates in 2020. The biggest white supremacist of them all is our current President, and the likes of George Soros, Bill Gates, and the other one percenters who run this government. White supremacy only exists because our politicians enjoy spreading misinformation about this topic.

Dennis Gravelle stated, "I believe we have people in our society that believe they are better than I. For me, I don't think that will ever change. White supremacy, to me, is just a political toy to get races to hate each other, and our politicians are idiots to spread hate in America. I feel that several individuals have remained in poverty with their political backing of the democrat party, who placed them into this position through their tyrannical legislation and restrictions for the community to succeed. Also, the false promises that were made that never came to fruition. I go to work daily and struggle just like my counterparts of other races that I see working hard just like me. I see black and white people working hand in hand to try and make a better life for themselves and their families. I would also like to expand on that. There are individuals of every race on this planet that believe they are better than everyone else. That goes for the white community, the black community, and the Asian and Hispanic communities. We will never be able to stop that in America."

Not only do we have white supremacists, but there are also black supremacists in our country. I found this article in Business and Politics (BPR) by Tom Tillson, called "Black Supremacist in Tulsa Rally," which preaches that it's time to 'kill everything white in sight' as revenge.

"While the Biden administration is preoccupied with a war on domestic terrorism, fueled by the mythical threat of white supremacy, and the FBI is busy chasing down "insurrectionists" who were supposedly trying to overthrow the government, extremist groups exist in America. Included among those groups are black nationalists who boldly declare in a public setting that the time will come when "black Americans will kill everything white in sight." A threat that was roundly ignored by the media establishment."

All races have people that hate others. Most of us don't feel we are better than anyone else. Here are the comments, we received on this question.

Deborah said, "There are people of all colors that think they are better than others! Most of us work hard for a living. Color doesn't enter into the equation. I feel it's more the elites of all colors who feel superior to those that have not, of all colors. White supremacy is an excuse for division."

Dorothy stated, "I totally agree. God created everyone equal and no one superior over any other."

Russell had this to say: "I totally agree. God created everyone equal and no one superior over any other."

***Elizabeth:*** *"I believe most White Supremacy claims in 2022 are nonexistent. I understand the World Economic Forum well enough to know that divisiveness is part of the plan to cause chaos needed to implement the New World Order A.K.A. The Great Reset. Food insecurity is another, so they are destroying food plants around the world. Also, job insecurity and money all blamed on "war," or this, that or the other, but all caused by them. Then they swoop in and offer to help with what they caused. Eventually they take the population down to 500,000,000 per the Georgia Guidestones."*

***Bruce:*** *"White supremacy is BS, I'm a wasp, (White Anglo Saxon Protestant) though I embrace the Church of God. I don't see color, race, religion, or sexual orientation, as long as you don't force any on me. I will stop and help anyone in the street. This is America, and despite what the fake news, or Liberals tell you, anyone can make something of their life if they study, and work hard."*

***Christopher:*** *"I'm gonna go as far as to say that racism doesn't exist, at least not in the modern sense, it's a made-up word from the left as a form of divisiveness. Just think of the current new word being tossed about transphobia. Another word created to shame individuals into accepting a lifestyle against their belief system. Therefore, if you don't agree with something you're automatically phobic or a racist. Democrats 3* *favorite words all ends in isms, bias and ists. Now I will acknowledge that individuals no matter their ethnicity or race hold and sometimes harbor biases, prejudices, and stereotypes but that's about as far as it goes."*

***Michael:*** *"White supremacy is all but dead. The Klan has all but disappeared and skinheads are extremely rare to encounter. But black centrism is still being taught and the Democrats do everything they can to keep people apart, including the new "wokeism". Without it they would go the way of the Whigs. Fortunately for the GOP, we have people like Mark Robinson, Winsome Sears, Tim Scott, and others who aren't afraid of being called Uncle Tom."*

Michael stated a great point when he mentioned the word "wokeism." This word has divided this country against each other, just like these politicians do again and again. Wokeism to most is a derogatory word and means: "aware of and actively attentive to important societal facts and issues (especially issues of racial and social justice). Maybe we should look at what the purpose of wokeism" is. We live in a country where citizens worry about offending someone else for something they have a strong opinion on, without realizing it. Then we have other individuals of this country that are waiting to be offended and immediately start the cancel process. We can't be afraid to speak our opinion. That is what makes us a great country.

*"Often used in contexts that suggest someone's expressed beliefs about such matters are not backed with genuine concern or action;* reflecting the attitudes of woke people; *disapproving: politically liberal (as in matters of racial and social justice) especially in a way that is considered unreasonable or extreme."* Racial and social issues are a very important topic but when corporations have woke policies, sending the wrong message to employees. Everyone wants to feel included, no matter what race, gender, or religious views we have. We can agree with that, but most of us want the freedom of opinion, and several people want to be left alone on this topic. When corporations shove this issue upon them, they take it personally. Several corporations have learned the hard way about going woke. People want this country to be more central, most don't want progressivism in their communities. "Maybe our corporate elite has finally woken up to the notion that it's bad business to piss off more than half the country with virtue-signaling progressive issues." By Charles Gasparino. People want to remain silent on wokeism, and they have the right to do

just that. Our so-called politicians have politicized wokeism, and we are afraid it may get worse. Look this topic up for yourself because knowledge is power.

***Robert:*** *"As long as there is welfare where minorities and women are predominant. The government is a master. By making these people dependent on them. Then the issue is not religious manipulation of society or white superiority. But the issue is slavery. Where the slaves see a society, they are not welcome to not by being lesser, but because they do not see a way to breach the barrier of being a slave to being a freeman. They been bought and sold and paid by the month.*

***Tamara:*** *"I think all races suffer from a certain amount of racism. I had a friend when I lived in Spain who was originally from Nigeria. Her father hated white people. I asked her once, why did your father move to a country whose majority is white if he hates white people. She just shrugged her shoulders. I think everyone in America has a chance of living a decent life. In fact, minorities sometimes have it easier. When I was in college looking for a scholarship, there were all sorts of scholarships that were solely based on color of skin and ethnicity but there was very little for a single white female like me who had just arrived in the country and was struggling to establish herself and go to college. Yes, some people are racist, but I don't believe the majority are. My personal dislike of a person has a lot more to do with how they act, in other words their fruit, what they might believe such as abortion, etc. than based on color or ethnicity."*

***Margaret:*** *"New World Order created the fake white supremacy paradigm to divide and conquer."*

***Marco:*** *"Yes, there is Trump time in office brought them out to the light he has empowered them."*

***Teresa:*** *"I definitely do not believe in white supremacy. And what is that name "white" even supposed to mean? My son, who is actually a reddish brown and freckled skinned, red headed male, and in 2007 didn't have a chance at a scholarship, but if he was a "black?" female, he would have been able to get all sorts of financial help. If anything, the government beats down on so called "white" males. Seen it often and it's so sad when an applicant with excellent skills for the job, gets turned down and hires a less qualified applicant instead only to meet a "racial" quota. When we divide or group people by their race, or job, or anything, we all lose. The government puts people in different boxes according to color, race, age, sex, etc. This causes division, not unity. No one person is any more, or any less important than the next. That includes actors, senators, representatives, judges, mayors, teachers' presidents, mothers, fathers, and on* *and on. We are all children of our loving Father who created each of us in His image, each Uniquely Different...no two are the same...That's who we are! It is literally useless to point out the differences of people...and then act with more respect or less...more per hour or less, etc. only due of those differences. That's what I see happening today. People are dividing by ideas and actions, race and color, thoughts, and beliefs, instead of looking at what we have in common. We need to be free to live our lives safely without doing harm to or being harmed by others and division is harming our world."*

Martin Luther King (MLK) envisioned a country that we could live together, not according to skin color, but by the content of their character. We have no clue why today, here in the year 2022 we are talking about white supremacy. If MLK were still alive we are sure he would be telling us to watch out for this government for they are the ones who we consider supremacists. It is not everyday workers of this society who are the racists, we leave that to politicians. We must find a way to unite this country and send a message to these so-called tyrants in office spreading a false narrative in society today. Don't forget the implementation of the administrative state started by Franklin Delano Roosevelt (FDR) who mandated three qualifications. 1. Be an expert, 2. Be untouchable by election and 3. Be a progressive.

*Lou: "I have a dream that my four little children will one day live in a nation where they will not be judged by the color of our skin, but by the content of that character." —MLK*

*"We were well on our way until we proved to the world how far we had come by voting in a black man as president of the USA, twice. This was the chance to become one, to realize MLK's words, but instead he divided us. The intervention of Trump held them off for four more years, but with the rigged election putting a senile fool into office the efforts to increase race division has reached epidemic levels. Consider a president who refers to over half of the citizens of the USA as semi-fascist and MAGA as the most extreme danger to our nation. Where having a Betsy Ross or Gadsden flag marks you as a White Supremacist. Where the FBI has been weaponized to intimidate, harass and destroy anyone the left considers an enemy. The only thing stopping them from complete take over is the 2nd amendment. History shows once they take your guns away, and they are trying to, it's game over. History shows time after time an unarmed civilian population is easy to control."*

**Wanda:** *"It's a political tool like you say. Most state prison systems have more white than black prisoners. Poverty is as prevalent in white areas as black like the hills of Kentucky and Tennessee and Appalachia and the mines of west Virginia...in the towns of the country that have the WRONG side of the tracks. Of the single white mothers that work two jobs to feed their kids because they can't get enough government aid and the thousands of white as well as black and Hispanic Americans homeless because of this corruption in our country.... color has nothing to do with poverty or wealth...."*

**Deborah:** *"There are people of all colors that think they are better than others! Most of us work hard for a living. Color doesn't enter into equation. I feel it's more the elites of all colors who feel superior to those that have not, of all colors. White supremacy is an excuse for division."*

**Dorothy:** *"I totally agree. God created everyone equal and no one superior over any other."*

**Lola:** *"A need to be superior is deeply rooted in our DNA. The growth of groups like the Nazis tells me that white supremacy exists and is gaining strength. It is like the devil. I believe it exists, but I don't worship it. There is no reason why we can't all work together and get along except for our own small, minded prejudices. The inequities built into our society are fueling divisions along race, religion, income, gender, age, etc. lines, pitting one group against another. As long as our attentions are focused on fighting each other, the root cause of all this will not be addressed as they should."*

**Margaret:** *"New World Order created the fake white supremacy paradigm to divide and conquer."*

**Johnny:** *"I never seen White Supremacy; they don't bother the Asian"*

**Bob:** *"The Democrat Party is using race to divide our country. They were the KKK many years ago. The poor blacks seem to fall for this, but it could be turning around because of the destruction of big Democrat Cities. All the theft you see in these cities is done primarily by poor black people caught on video. This started when Trump was President but continues out of control under Biden's Administration. They don't know how to fix this or anything else. They just want to throw money at everything, because it gets used as dark money for their candidates. Theft!"*

**Ruben:** *"We have a narcissistic, pathological liar that the only reason he can't give up that he lost the presidential election. he is not accepting his and dividing the country."*

The comment that Ruben just stated we can't disagree with that statement. Here we are just a few weeks after the midterm election and Trump has already announced he is running to be our next president. Already in the media he met with a man whom the Justice Department has called Nick Fuentes at his Mar-a-Lago estate in Florida. He also met with Kanye West who also used antisemitic comments in the past. We have no clue why a man who is trying to be our president again is meeting with racist people. You can read this story called Trump met with white supremacist Nick Fuentes alongside Ye at Mar-A-Lago, by Zach Schoenfeld. Ye is what West goes by now. You can't make this up. We have said it before, and we will say it again, the racist people here in America are the very rich white and black people who run our country. Trump should be ashamed of himself and rethink the way he should run for president. We can't wait to hear the coverup on this one.

**Katlynn:** *"I think white supremacy only exists in certain bubbles these days and in the minds of politicians and other race baiting groups. I also know for a fact that black supremacy is on the rise, and it is sad to see. I think no race is supreme and that we are all created equal as God says. There is simply good and evil in this world, and I wish all the racism towards every race would just stop."*

**Bruce:** *"There is one race the human race."*

We can all agree with Bruce. Maybe someday everyone here in America, this great country we live in will realize there is only one race, "the human race." Next people express their views on climate change. Man is flawed and the evil that resides in Washington, D.C. feeds off our weakness for their own benefit. Educate yourself with the founding of your government and try to experience the miracles of our creator. Read on Patriots!

# Chapter 7

# "Climate Change"

Do you believe in global warming, or is it just a lie by our government to scare people?

I am sure most of us older Americans like Jack and myself remember the name Al Gore, He was Vice-President Under Bill Clinton during the 90s, yes way back when. Back in 1993, Gore told us that climate change was happening due to rising temperatures. Even today he is telling anyone who'll listen that climate change is still a major factor today. For thirty years we have been hearing that climate change will affect the USA unless we take the bull by the horns to combat this issue. This was in 1993, "The majority of scientists have been telling us for years that the long-term warming trend greatly increases the odds that any given year will produce a much larger number of 100-degree days," Gore said. That is true, we did have hot weather in 1993, according to data. We have also had cold winters in the United States, that no one, even the media is talking about.

In 2022 Gore was back in the news with more on climate change blaming governments for not doing enough, telling us that leaders have a credibility problem regarding the climate. "We have a credibility problem all of us: We're talking and we're starting to act, but we're not doing enough," Gore said during a speech at the opening ceremony of the summit. "We must see the so-called 'dash for gas' for what it really is: a dash down a bridge to nowhere, leaving the countries of the world facing climate chaos and billions in stranded assets, especially here in Africa. We have to move beyond the era of fossil fuel colonialism." He said those comments at a November 2022 COP29 climate conference. Thirty years ago, Mr. Gore started talking about climate change, more like forty years ago, but who's counting? Gore has been screaming from the rooftops about rising sea levels and the destruction of America. Then he buys a mansion on the west coast which is where sea levels are supposed to rise the most. That would be the first place to go under the ocean. We find this amazing; do you really think he believes in global warming or does he do it for the huge contracts he has? According to data we looked up, the Pacific Ocean since 1990 increased two to three times the global average. But he still bought a house on the ocean.

This isn't the first time someone has predicted when the world was going to end, Gore just happens to be the first to say it about climate change. We'll just mention a few. In the year 1910, HALLEY'S COMET would crash into earth. Then in 2000, people thought the world was going to end then with Y2K. We were told it was an impending apocalypse. In 2012 it was the MAYAN calendar that would lead us to our demise. Guess what, everyone, none of those events happened. Halley's Comet never crashed, Y2K came and went, and the Mayan calendar was wrong. Everyone who predicted the demise of America was totally wrong, so why do people believe in climate change now, when Gore has been saying it for more than thirty years? There is only one supreme being that knows when the world is going to end and that is the Almighty God. No one else does. These predictions are made to scare the hell out of people, and it really does. This issue has caused as much division in this country as other major issues like voting, the economy, and immigration. 48% of people in the United States believe in global warming. Then why do presidents buy oceanfront property? Can you see where it's hard to believe this is a reality?

We believe that global warming, the new name for climate change is just a political issue. Again, to scare voting constituents that they must follow one political party over the other. In 2019 Rep. Alexandria Ocasio-Cortez (D-N.Y.) said she thinks that there in an urgency needed in addressing man-made climate change, warning that it will "destroy the planet" in a dozen years if humans do not address the issue, no matter the cost. That means in 2031 we will finally face the end of humanity. Politicians are supposed to be leaders and inform everyone that we live in the greatest country ever created, instead of telling us that she only talks about destruction of this nation. These are the kind of people we are electing to political office, people who believe we are heading for extinction. I am going to go out on a limb and say, in 2031 and 2032 and beyond we will still be living in the greatest country ever. We need two things in this country, optimism, and faith, not a pessimist. After researching this topic, I find it funny that only one democrat is telling us that we have only a dozen years left on this earth. What does that tell you? Sounds like a hoax and political stunt to us.

Over the past 30 plus years we have heard about this topic and yet we are still here and still hearing about climate change and global warming. We don't see it ending anytime soon. Most people need to understand that our climate is very complex here on earth and yet several people think they have figured it out, they haven't. Climate change is interdisciplinary and takes many years to study. It takes many disciplines and tools to figure our climate out. When Jack and I were kids growing up in New York and during the hottest days in June thru August you know what term we used for those days? We called it summer, and when we had beautiful days in September and October, we called that an Indian summer. No one wants to know what we called the frigid days in winter, the name wouldn't be right for a book, but we are sure you know what we mean. No one ever said we're having a climate cooling or another Ice Age, except during the 70s. The reason why is because another Ice Age doesn't fit the scare scenario.

The comments we received on this topic showed us how people are fed up with global warming. Here are some of those comments.

*Jim: "The planet warms, the planet cools. it is cyclical and has nothing to do with taxing humanity into the stone age for the benefit of a very few (I'm talking to you, Al Gore). look past short-term wobbles, to million-year trends. toss the fear mongers and thieves out on their ears. if they are sweating global warming, move them to Antarctica."*

*Marilyn: "Mother Nature is all. The weather is going to be what it will be. We are just here to experience it. There is not much we can do other than be better prepared for them when they come. These climate cultists just learned how to capitalize upon it. Kind of like the TV evangelists of years ago. same thing. Additionally, what good is what we do here in this country if nobody else abides in the rest of the world? I'm not saying anything new. But We must have super-duper egos if we actually think anything that we do is going to really make a significant change in this enormous solar system that we live in."*

*Janet: "There is no such thing as global warming, climate change or whatever the liberal liars are calling it these days."*

**Christopher:** *"The only truth to any reality concerning climate change is deforestation."*

**Hakon:** *"Before we can discuss "global warming" you must first educate yourself on the cycles of the last 5 ice ages. This is the 5th ice age that we are living in now and it's coming to an end. According to the data from the last 4 (as noted by geologists) it will be marked by a constant global climb in temperature until it reaches a pinacol then drops rabidly back down into the next ice age. This happens over the course of tens of thousands of years. This ice age began its climb about 25 thousand years ago. In a few thousand years it will slam down into another freezing ice age. The differences between the climb of this ice age compared to the last 4 is perceptible but not really notable. This is not opinion; this is scientific fact."*

**Kathy:** *"Do you remember the hole in the ozone? And acid rain? Another scare tactic by the government Look at California. Can an average person working pay 6.00 a gallon for gas. No. But can an average person buy an electric car that will cost more than a gas car plus the charging on the electric grid. Which at this time runs on fossil fuels. I can go on and on."*

**Nicholas:** *"Lies perpetrated by a media that is owned by anti-Christians who are organizing genocide against us."*

**Bettye:** *"I am 81 years old and have been hearing about ice age and global warming etc. etc. forever. Nothing has changed in 200 years. We warm a little sometimes and then cool. Everything gets blamed on global warming, but we have been having tornados and hurricanes for at least 200 years. The people making the claims are just wanting to make themselves rich and they do all the things that we are told not to do."*

**Ben:** *"So many things wrong with how this Democratic agenda is being rammed down our throats. - Climate Change is Debatable; man causing it is even more debatable... for the moment I'll not contest. - What is the strategy and plans for any of this? Other than spending Billions... soon to be Trillions. What is the plan?- I have seen NO PLAN! Zero!- Why are we not putting whatever the new solution is going to be in place BEFORE we pull the rug out from under existing energy? - Basic question: When we eliminate all fossil fuel use (cars, home heating, power plants) - how much 'clean' energy do we need? - How will this be generated - wind, solar, nuclear? - Solar farms take thousands of acres... how many square miles of land and sea is required? Where will they be built?- How will cars in urban areas with on street parking charge? Charging stations all along the streets? Will they be private, or* *government managed?- Have environmental studies been done?- How many, where from will the batteries come? - No basic answers, No strategy, and No Plan.- The start of this hysteria was a 2018 UN report (the science) which states: "Without increased and urgent mitigation ambition in the coming years, leading to a sharp decline in greenhouse gas emissions by 2030, global warming will surpass 1.5° C in the following decades, leading to irreversible loss of the most fragile ecosystems, and crisis after crisis for the most vulnerable people and societies." End of World! 2030! This 'science' was used by AOC as the basis for this madness - see AOC's 2019 R.Res.109!"*

What Ben is referring to is this.

116TH CONGRESS

1ST SESSION H. RES. ____

*Recognizing the duty of the Federal Government to create a Green New Deal.*

**IN THE HOUSE OF REPRESENTATIVES**

Ms. OCASIO-CORTEZ submitted the following resolution; which was re-ferred to

the Committee on ______

RESOLUTION

**Recognizing the duty of the Federal Government to create a Green New Deal.**

*Whereas* the October 2018 report entitled "Special Report on Global Warming of 1.5oC" by the intergovernmental Panel on Climate Change and the November 2018 Fourth National Climate Assessment report found that—

human activity is the dominant cause of observed climate change over the past century;

a changing climate is causing sea levels to rise and an increase in wildfires, severe storms, droughts, and other extreme weather events that threaten human life, healthy communities, and critical infrastructure

global warming at or above 2 degrees Celsius beyond pre-industrialized levels will cause—

mass migration from the regions most affected by climate change;

more than $500,000,000,000 in lost annual economic output in the United States by the year 2100;

wildfires that, by 2050, will annually burn at least twice as much forest area in the western United States than was typically burned by wildfires in the years preceding 2019;

a loss of more than 99 percent of all coral reefs on Earth;

more than 350,000,000 more people to be exposed globally to deadly heat stress by 2050; and

a risk of damage to $1,000,000,000,000,000 of public infrastructure and coastal real estate in the United States; and

global temperatures must be kept below 1.5 degrees Celsius above pre-industrialized levels to avoid the most severe impacts of a changing climate, which will require—

global reductions in greenhouse gas emissions from human sources of 40 to 60 percent from 2010 levels by 2030; and

net-zero emissions by 2050;

*Whereas*, because the United States has historically been responsible for a disproportionate amount of greenhouse gas emissions, having emitted 20 percent of global greenhouse gas emissions through 2014, and has a high technological capacity, the United States must take a leading role in reducing emissions through economic transformation;

*Whereas* the United States is currently experiencing several related crises, with—

life expectancy declining while basic needs, such as clean air, clean water, healthy food, and adequate health care, housing, transportation, and education, are inaccessible to a significant portion of the United States population;

a 4-decade trend of economic stagnation, deindustrialization, and anti-labor policies that has led to—

hourly wages overall stagnating since the 1970s despite increased worker productivity;

the third-worst level of socioeconomic mobility in the developed world before the Great Recession

the erosion of the earning and bargaining power of workers in the United States; and

inadequate resources for public sector workers to confront the challenges of climate change at local, State, and Federal levels; and

the greatest income inequality since the 1920s, with—

the top 1 percent of earners accruing 91percent of gains in the first few years of economic recovery after the Great Recession;

a large racial wealth divide amounting to a difference of 20 times more wealth between the average White family and the average Black family; and

a gender earnings gap that results in women earning approximately 80 percent as much as men, at the median;

*Whereas* climate change, pollution, and environmental destruction have exacerbated systemic racial, regional, social, environmental, and economic injustices (referred to in this preamble as "systemic injustices") by disproportionately affecting indigenous communities, communities of color, migrant communities, deindustrialized communities, depopulated rural communities, the poor, low-income workers, women, the elderly, the unhoused, people with disabilities, and youth (referred to in this preamble as "frontline and vulnerable communities");

*Whereas,* climate change constitutes a direct threat to the national security of the United States—

by impacting the economic, environmental, and social stability of countries and communities around the world; and

by acting as a threat multiplier;

*Whereas* the Federal Government-led mobilizations during World War II and the New Deal created the greatest middle class that the United States has ever seen, but many members of frontline and vulnerable communities were excluded from many of the economic and societal benefits of those mobilizations; and

*Whereas* the House of Representatives recognizes that a new national, social, industrial, and economic mobilization on a scale not seen since World War II and the New Deal is a historic opportunity—

to create millions of good, high-wage jobs in the United States;

to provide unprecedented levels of prosperity and economic security for all people of the United States; and

to counteract systemic injustices:

Now, therefore, be it

**Resolved,** That it is the sense of the House of Representatives that—

it is the duty of the Federal Government to create a Green New Deal—

to achieve net-zero greenhouse gas emissions through a fair and just transition for all communities and workers;

to create millions of good, high-wage jobs and ensure prosperity and economic security for all people of the United States;

to invest in the infrastructure and industry of the United States to sustainably meet the challenges of the 21st century;

to secure for all people of the United States for generations to come—
(i) clean air and water;

(ii) climate and community resiliency;

(iii) healthy food;

(iv) access to nature; and

(v) a sustainable environment; and

to promote justice and equity by stopping current, preventing future, and repairing historic oppression of indigenous communities, communities of color, migrant communities, deindustrialized communities, depopulated rural communities, the poor, low-income workers, women, the elderly, the unhoused, people with disabilities, and youth (referred to in this resolution as "frontline and vulnerable communities");

the goals described in subparagraphs of paragraph (1) above (referred to in this resolution as the "Green New Deal goals") should be accomplished through a 10-year national mobilization (referred to in this resolution as the "Green New Deal mobilization") that will require the following goals and projects—

building resiliency against climate change-related disasters, such as extreme weather, including by leveraging funding and providing investments for community-defined projects and strategies;

repairing and upgrading the infrastructure in the United States, including—
(i) by eliminating pollution and greenhouse gas emissions as much as technologically feasible;

(ii) by guaranteeing universal access to clean water;

(iii) by reducing the risks posed by flooding and other climate impacts; and

(iv) by ensuring that any infrastructure bill considered by Congress addresses climate change;

meeting 100 percent of the power demand in the United States through clean, renewable, and zero-emission energy sources, including—

(i) by dramatically expanding and upgrading existing renewable power sources; and

(ii) by deploying new capacity;

building or upgrading to energy-efficient, distributed, and "smart" power grids, and working to ensure affordable access to electricity;

upgrading all existing buildings in the United States and building new buildings to achieve maximal energy efficiency, water efficiency, safety, affordability, comfort, and durability, including through electrification;

spurring massive growth in clean manufacturing in the United States and removing pollution and greenhouse gas emissions from manufacturing and industry as much as is technologically feasible, including by expanding renewable energy manufacturing and investing in existing manufacturing and industry;

working collaboratively with farmers and ranchers in the United States to eliminate pollution and greenhouse gas emissions from the agricultural sector as much as is technologically feasible, including—

(i) by supporting family farming;

(ii) by investing in sustainable farming and land use practices that increase soil health; and

(iii) by building a more sustainable food system that ensures universal access to healthy food;

overhauling transportation systems in the United States to eliminate pollution and greenhouse gas emissions from the transportation sector as much as is technologically feasible, including through investment in—

(i) zero-emission vehicle infrastructure and manufacturing;

(ii) clean, affordable, and accessible public transportation; and

(iii) high-speed rail;

mitigating and managing the long-term adverse health, economic, and other effects of pollution and climate change, including by providing funding for community-defined projects and strategies;

removing greenhouse gases from the atmosphere and reducing pollution, including by restoring natural ecosystems through proven low-tech solutions that increase soil carbon storage, such as preservation and afforestation;

restoring and protecting threatened, endangered, and fragile ecosystems through locally appropriate and science-based projects that enhance biodiversity and support climate resiliency;

cleaning up existing hazardous waste and abandoned sites to promote economic development and sustainability;

identifying other emission and pollution sources and creating solutions to eliminate them; and

promoting the international exchange of technology, expertise, products, funding, and services, with the aim of making the United States the international leader on climate action, and to help other countries achieve a Green New Deal;

a Green New Deal must be developed through transparent and inclusive consultation, collaboration, and partnership with frontline and vulnerable communities, labor unions, worker cooperatives, civil society groups, academia, and businesses; and

to achieve the Green New Deal goals and mobilization, a Green New Deal will require the following goals and projects—

providing and leveraging, in a way that ensures that the public receives appropriate ownership stakes and returns on investment, adequate capital (including through community grants, public banks, and other public financing), technical expertise, supporting policies, and other forms of assistance to communities, organizations, Federal, State, and local government agencies, and businesses working on the Green New Deal mobilization;

ensuring that the Federal Government takes into account the complete environmental and social costs and impacts of emissions through—
(i) existing laws;
(ii) new policies and programs; and
(iii) ensuring that frontline and vulnerable communities shall not be adversely affected;

providing resources, training, and high-quality education, including higher education, to all people of the United States, with a focus on frontline and vulnerable communities, so those communities may be full and equal participants in the Green New Deal mobilization;

making public investments in the research and development of new clean and renewable energy technologies and industries;

directing investments to spur economic development, deepen and diversify industry in local and regional economies, and build wealth and community ownership, while prioritizing high-quality job creation and economic, social, and environmental benefits in frontline and vulnerable communities that may otherwise struggle with the transition away from greenhouse gas intensive industries;

ensuring the use of democratic and participatory processes that are inclusive of and led by frontline and vulnerable communities and workers to plan, implement, and administer the Green New Deal mobilization at the local level;

ensuring that the Green New Deal mobilization creates high-quality union jobs that pay prevailing wages, hires local workers, offers training and advancement opportunities, and guarantees wage and benefit parity for workers affected by the transition;

guaranteeing a job with a family-sustaining wage, adequate family and medical leave, paid vacations, and retirement security to all people of the United States;

strengthening and protecting the right of all workers to organize, unionize, and collectively bargain free of coercion, intimidation, and harassment;

strengthening and enforcing labor, workplace health and safety, antidiscrimination, and wage and hour standards across all employers, industries, and sectors;

enacting and enforcing trade rules, procurement standards, and border adjustments with strong labor and environmental protections—
(i) to stop the transfer of jobs and pollution overseas; and
(ii) to grow domestic manufacturing in the United States;

ensuring that public lands, waters, and oceans are protected and that eminent domain is not abused;

obtaining the free, prior, and informed consent of indigenous people for all decisions that affect indigenous people and their traditional territories, honoring all treaties and agreements with indigenous people, and protecting and enforcing the sovereignty and land rights of indigenous people;

ensuring a commercial environment where every businessperson is free from unfair competition and domination by domestic or international monopolies; and

providing all people of the United States with—
(i) high-quality health care;
(ii) affordable, safe, and adequate housing;

(iii) economic security; and

(iv) access to clean water, clean air, healthy and affordable food, and nature.

It looks like her resources come out of two committees. Where are the facts? Committees are just people's opinions. How does this connect to life in America right now? We still must live our lives and make the best out of what we have. We just want to mention one thing that we the people are good at. That is rebuilding after a major catastrophe. No matter what happens, being a flood, tornado, fire in our forests, or our cities being leveled after a hurricane or earthquake, we bounce back and make it better. We have seen it repeatedly, we come back stronger and better with more ideas on how we make us safer just in case it happens again. Every line in this Green New Deal talks about despair and we can't recover after a loss. Here in South Carolina, we have been through two hurricanes and one major flood over the past 7 years and each community has pulled through. Are there some families that get displaced and can't recover, yes, but those are the ones that should receive more assistance from the federal government.

**Doug:** *"Our Planet Earth wobbles on its axis changing its pitch to the sun causing theses changes in our climate and has gone back and forth with temperatures changes for millions and millions of years! All caused naturally! That's why we have had several Ice Ages! What we are doing here with fuels and everything else we use to live off of has very little to nothing to do with any of it! All of the crap the corrupt liberal, leftist, socialist, racist, communist politicians and their supporters are telling us are lies folks! Especially about climate change! And check it out folks for yourselves! We have already been through the warmest part of our current climate change cycle! We are cooler now then we were in 1934!"*

**Christopher:** *"I have no doubt about the reality of climate change. I have HUGE doubts about the government explanations and proposed solutions. Yes, panic mongering to expand government power."*

**Jon:** *"We have deserts where there were forests, we had ice that covered north America, the earth has warmed and cooled since the beginning of time it's just another weather pattern in earth's history, there is NOTHING we as humans can do to change it."*

**Bud:** *"Proven fact that the earth and the sun effect our climate…… not man."*

**Edmund:** *"It is called WEATHER… and it happens regardless what stupid humans do…. unless they unleash a Nuclear Winter in the Ukraine, like loser Putin* *is threatening to do... that is MUCH MORE dangerous than cow farts or automobile exhaust."*

**Denise:** *"The entire Climate Change alarm is a scam to make money for the various groups that funnel it to the elitists that head these organizations. They now control so much power, they're forcing corporations to change their methods in order to get financing for making any improvements. BlackRock is notorious for this. It's called ESG. Vanguard is also guilty. The entire green movement/environmental movement has been weaponized, including the EPA.*

**Rene:** *"The earth is constantly changing...self-adapting...mother nature is very tricky...it will always find a way. I remember Walter Cronkite reporting on a new ice age back in the 70s...so I am in agreement with you. It is a way to move our tax dollars around and feed it to ppl that align with them. Like what was the solar company that Obama gave monies too? Where are they? Exactly..."*

**David:** *""Hoax" lol. Science is hard. Conspiracy theories are so much easier."*

**Pearl:** *"I think it's a money maker for those like Al Gore. They use flawed science that they created to measure "climate change". We need to be good stewards of our earth however while they are telling us to cut down on emissions and they are jetting around the world in private jets…they don't need to speak to me. They want our oil resources reduced while they buy from those who don't care about emissions, while we can produce for ourselves cleaner and safer. They are all a bunch of rich thugs that cares about nothing but padding their pockets."*

The following comments are from individuals who believe that the United States does have a global warming/climate change problem. That is what they feel and have strong convictions on it. The great part about the good ole USA is that we can have a difference of opinion and I respect them for that opinion. That is what makes this country great.

**Darin:** *"It's definitely possible, we watched California go from having a January-February monsoon season to having fires in those months and it only took a few short years. Whether it's a warming trend and we're fine or a more urgent matter, it's been yet another narrative for the better part of a century that many have peddled for profit, control, or both."*

**Linda:** *"Humans have / are doing great harm to the environment - how can all these changes not be connected to us. Our products and by-products affect the earth's* *ability to heal itself. We humans don't give it a running chance —- which means we humans are done for."*

**Anonymous:** *"Global warming has been happening since before mankind. Where I live was under 1 mile of ice. Thousands of us have installed Weather Flow Tempest equipment to monitor weather. It shows no IMMEDIATE GLOBAL THREAT … look it up, Google Tempest Weather."*

We all realize that these new outlets and weather stations can't be trusted to report correctly so we should have our own weather station where we as individuals check for accurate forecasts. It is your own home weather system. He may be onto something here. Just look up Tempest Weather.

**Diane:** *"The earth has been engaged in climate changes for eons of time. There is nothing that will stop it from happening. There is no harm in practical behaviors if you think it will contribute to a better climate, providing those methods do not unnecessarily infringe on others."*

**Geneva:** *"Today's climate monitoring systems are lightyears ahead of the ones we had in the Seventies - and the Earth has warmed a lot since then, about the same amount as predicted by the greenhouse gases emitted in the meantime, only more so at the poles. You are correct that if the natural cycles had continued with no human interference, we *would* need to be worrying about another Ice Age! However, the only opinions that really count on this issue are those of climate scientists or people who live in places that are rapidly becoming uninhabitable because of the changing climate.*

**James:** *"Global warming is a fact. Period."*

**Bruce:** *"It's happening. Your grandchildren will pay for our mistakes."*

**James:** *"Man made greenhouse gas are having an effect on the Earths atmosphere, what the actual result of that effect will be, we do not know for sure. Yet we know it is changing the atmosphere."*

**Annie:** *"I am a gardener. When I moved to CA in the 90's and was putting a garden in, I noticed that every plant I put into full sun (because that's what it needs) died. The sun was unbelievably hot. I know that it's not snowing nearly as much in the northeast as it was when I moved here 15 years ago. It's more like CT. Yes, I believe we are killing this planet. We are destroying earth's life blood by fooling around with its life support system. This will take some time. It won't happen in a few years. What* *harm does it do to clean up our act? Why not do it? Cancer rates are through the roof. In animals also. Why s—t in our own home?*

*Clyde: "Aside from the hysterical debate, there is a consensus that humans do have an effect on warming of the earth, but not to the degree that the climate alarmists claim. I believe you are correct about the temperatures rising and falling over a period of years. In the past, I have read about the affects of the solar cycle on our climate. It has been several years, so the details escape me."*

*Paul: "I believe in it because I've seen the weather pattern change in my neck of the woods, this is my lake, should be up around tree line, never been this low in 35 years. I get earth goes through changes, but we can't keep dumping crap into air and water, without repercussions or speeding up the process."*

We do understand that weather changes constantly. Our country will not be destroyed by our climate like politicians want us to believe, they will destroy our economy from the inside. If these politicians really care about rising oceans and major hurricanes, why do they, along with famous people and activists own oceanfront beach houses? The climate czar John Kerry who flies around the world in his private jet is telling us we need to do our part in saving our environment. Give me a break. Just to mention a few who do own houses who say that climate change is real are; Barack Obama owns a home in Martha's Vineyard, on the ocean; even President Biden has a mansion on the beach in Delaware. If that doesn't tell you it's a hoax, then we are too late in reaching you. The last quote sums up climate change in layman's terms and is nicely stated.

*Cindi: "Climate change is weather, and it's been changing for billions of years. Weather is weather."*

Our next chapter we get into statistics about crime and how people feel on this political issue. Stay with us, Patriots!

# Chapter 8

# "Crime in America"

Is crime a serious problem where you live? City, town, or state?
Do the police do a good job in your country?
Is carrying a gun a good way to stay safe? Why or why not?
Do you think the world will be safer or more dangerous in the future?
What were the main causes for our increase in crime across America?

At the end of November 2022, the midterm elections had just concluded. One topic that voters were concerned about was Crime in America. We have always had crime here and we always will. There are individuals out there who believe they should have things that others have and not pay for them. We have evil people living here and that will never change. The problem with crime is that it all starts with politicians on both sides of the aisle. Democrat politicians like Alexandra Ocasio Cortez (AOC), and Maxine Waters tell crowds they should break the law, get in people's faces especially when they are in restaurants, and tell them they are not welcome. AOC recently talked about Supreme Court Judge Kavanaugh being harassed in a restaurant telling us that she basically supports the violation of people's rights. In their minds, they think it's all right to make waves because they dislike police officers, but we are sure that the first people they call when help is needed are the police. Republican politicians are just as bad, they remain silent and let cities get rioted and burned. They say it's only democrat-run cities, so why should we worry about what they do there? The only ones that end up hurt from their lack of ability to act are the victims. Not one of our political clowns has any solutions to the rising crime and violence happening every day in this country. Just blame the other party and the people buy it.

These days, people are scared to leave their homes and won't send their children outside to play. We have become a rotten society created by politicians who fail us more and more and more. Instead of holding people accountable for their actions when they commit a crime, these politicians create legislation going after law-abiding citizens by restricting their right to carry a firearm which is a right in our United States Constitution. Under the Bill of Rights Amendment II it states, "A well-regulated Militia, being necessary to the security of a free State, the right of the people to keep and bear Arms, shall not be infringed." What the hell is happening, people?

The problem is that bad guys will always get guns from gangs, cartels, and pissed-off gun dealers.

But the solution for them is taking away guns from law-abiding citizens. That's their answer to crime. How stupid does that sound? Let's not prosecute the criminal, let's take people's guns away.

In every state, in every city, they have a problem with gangs, guns, and violence. We already know our 2nd Amendment Rights are the hardest to keep. Having a right is your right, you shouldn't have to jump through hoops to practice a constitutional right. If we let this government restrain any of our rights, where will they stop? We must remember that we the people have voted these hacks into office, and we've kept them in for decades, so whose fault is it? District attorneys also need to be held accountable for the jobs they are doing, most of them poorly.

That is republican and democrat DAs not doing their jobs to prosecute quality-of-life crimes.

What are quality-of-life crimes? Most cities have municipal laws for law enforcement to be able to arrest. They are loitering, disorderly conduct, shoplifting, simple assaults, and driving offenses such as DWI and other traffic stops. The last time we looked, driving in the United States is a privilege, not a right. Politicians have lost sight of that. We even have states that restrict officers from stopping cars, how asinine is that?

These statistics are from 2019 on all offenses committed that year. There were over ten million crimes. That ranges from murder to property crimes. But the only crime we hear about is murder and mass shooting, the rest of these crimes, if prosecuted, would not have led to violent crime. Therefore, district attorneys should prosecute for quality-of-life crimes. Politicians in general want us to believe that law enforcement only picks on the black community and want us to believe that we are a racist country. Check out these numbers and it shows a different outcome, and people have always told me numbers don't lie. Politicians have been creating divisions within three ethnic groups, and that is White, Black, and Asian.

Here they are, curfew and loitering 14,650 crimes so let's break it down by race and the number of arrests for each crime committed.

| White | Black | Indian and Asian |
|---|---|---|
| 9640 | 4380 | 260 |

Simple assaults were 1,025,710 of that year. Broken down by race.

| White | Black | Indian and Asian |
|---|---|---|
| 66,4630 | 31,9920 | 17,780 |

The last statistic we will check is weapons because that's the problem American politicians want us to believe. These are carrying and possession offences for a grand total of 153,160.

| White | Black | Indian and Asian |
|---|---|---|
| 85,120 | 64,070 | 2,380 |

That is the total number of arrests made for 2019 for White, Black, and Asian individuals. I am sure most of them were never prosecuted due to lackluster district attorneys. A prime example of not holding people accountable is right here in South Carolina. Most prosecutors won't charge violators with DUI, they let them plead down to avoid trials. That is a slap in the face of (MADD), Mothers Against Drunk Driving, who feel people should be placed in jail for this specific violation. So, now this person is out of jail and able to drive drunk again with the possibility of serious injury not only to themselves but to others as well. All because these DAs won't do their job, it's easier to give a fine than prepare for a court trial. Why do we bring this up? The answer is simple. Not prosecuting quality-of-life crimes leads to more violent crimes in our society, like motor vehicle theft, aggravated assaults, rape, robbery, and MURDER. This is the number one reason why we need to hold people accountable. Prosecuting quality-of-life crimes reduces the chance of violent crimes. It's that plain and simple. Do the job you were elected to do or get the hell out. That's all failing politicians and district attorneys. We know who you are, which is most of you, republican and democrat. People are starting to wake up and soon will be UNITED and you, the politician, will be done.

The federal government creates this illusion that people of color commit the most crimes. They like to use percentages instead of numbers. Currently, in this country, we have 232 million White people, 62.57 million Hispanic people, an Indian population of 4.46 million individuals, and the Black community, a total population of 41.6 million people. Of course, when you use percentage points the Black community having the smallest population will have a higher percentage relating to crime. The group that commits the most crimes is the white population. The sad part is that many Americans fall for this false narrative. We believe that anyone who commits a crime should receive some sort of punishment to let them know that form of behavior will not be tolerated. If the person wants to commit another crime, jail must be the option. In my experience as a corrections officer, very few who commit crimes become rehabilitated and become productive members of society. Unfortunately, the voice of the victim is being lost and getting harder to hear and they usually reside in the neediest neighborhoods since most crimes are crimes of opportunity. To reduce crime, communities must start prosecuting these quality-of-life crimes; it helps citizens feel safer. If they don't see a drug pusher on the street corner, or the 3-card Monty, or the guy on the street corner who jumps out at you to wash your windshield, citizens feel the police are doing their jobs. Today, politicians and activists say they want to defund the police for the way they believe they act while on duty. The first budget cut will be in the training of officers, and that is what activists say police need. That will affect generations in policing.

I (Dennis) hated statistics when I was in high school and college, barely passing any math classes. Today, for some reason I finally understand why numbers matter. Social justice reform, people, and news media organizations tell us that there is a higher percentage of blacks in prisons, so we decided to look up more statistics. We went to the Federal Bureau of Prisons and found the following percentages. These numbers reflect 2007-2017, which is a 10-year period. At the end of that period, federal and state prisons had 475,900 incarcerated black inmates or 33 percent, 436,500 white inmates, 30 percent, only a small difference of about 140,000 between the two races. In a country of over 300 million individuals, that is not a huge number. The Hispanic population was 338,500 or 23 percent of total inmates. The numbers are closer than what politicians have been telling us. We wouldn't expect anything less from these tyrants we have in office.

The point we are trying to make here is that when percentages are used the Black community seems to get the raw deal, but, like we said earlier, numbers don't lie. The Black community has a lower number of Americans, so using percentages will always make it look like the Black community suffers more. We are not saying they don't suffer, what we are saying is that we must find the core problem of why criminals commit the crimes they do. Not just in the Black community, but in all communities. Remember our vice president who oversees the border said, regarding immigration told U.S. citizens that she wants to stop the root causes of why immigrants cross the border. She didn't do well with that and when it comes to crimes in our streets, not only she, but every politician has failed to address this major issue. Jack stated that "The problem with today's politicians is that police officers treat the poor neighborhood with a different principle. Now being retired from the law enforcement community, I don't believe that; at least not with the terrific officers I worked with. I do know that is the light today's politicians like to put on law enforcement, but why? Because this is a hot topic that divides the American people." We will get more into this later in this chapter. Let's see what some of we the people had to say about these five questions I asked.

*Jim:* "*I live in Columbia SC.*

*1. Is crime a serious problem where you live? City, town, or state? Answer: Not as much violent crimes as there is a theft problem. And doesn't seem to be getting any better.*

*2. Do the police do a good job in your country? Answer: Underfunded and under trained law enforcement has always struggled with the abuse of power - tyranny is created in the shadowed unconscious psyche of otherwise powerless individuals see: toxic environmental exposure*

*3. Is carrying a gun a good way to stay safe? Why or why not? Answer: Being armed should improve the outcome of any violent situation. The right to bare arms must be protected to secure all other individual human rights imo (in my opinion).*

*4. Do you think the world will be safer or more dangerous in the future? Should get more violent as despot behaviors from the evermore growing desperate citizens in societies from the toxic sociological impact from our experiences that is a feed forward feedback environmental exposure in our evermore competitiveness over resources in the marketplace.*

*5. What were the main causes for our increase in crime across America? Answer: Stressful environment  . Poor dietary habits - nutritional deficiencies (see: inflationary economic climate/disenfranchised citizens). Inflationary economic climate. Overly aggressive prosecutorial legal system. Disenfranchised citizens.*

**Nick:** *"Crime in America"*

*1. Is crime a serious problem where you live? City, town, or state? "I live in Texas. Not huge here but it is growing."*

*2. Do the police do a good job in your country? Overall, was there support for the police yes. Were their hands handcuffed behind their back not so much. Let's not discuss the politicized police and Federal Law enforcement. They are doing a horrid job.*

*3. Is carrying a gun a good way to stay safe? Why or why not? I believe it is. I don't carry but I am glad others do. Citizens on the scene of many crimes have stopped that. I feel every citizen should be required to be trained in firearm safety and use even it they do not carry ever.*

*4. Do you think the world will be safer or more dangerous in the future? If we continue the constant divisiveness, then way more dangerous. I don't see and end to the divisiveness either. Not yet.*

*5. What were the main causes for our increase in crime across America? Public endorsement of crime by the so-called leaders of the nation has spurred it on. When the VP of the United States helps to fund a bailout program of violent criminals that speak volumes to criminal elements. When cashless bail or release without bail of violent criminals is policy that too speaks volumes to criminals. When it becomes legal to shoplift that is a huge one to speak to criminals.*

**Jeff:** *Hello Dennis, thanks for joining my group. I do think crime is a serious problem in many parts of our country and government. This BS about minimizing the prison population and cash free bail makes it all worse. People commit crimes and there is no accountability in many highly populated cities. I live in rural America and crime is treated differently and more traditionally such that you commit a crime you go to jail post bail and follow a legal process that holds one accountable. I do not see the logic of what the left intends for our country to become creating this nontraditional criminal process. Then there is the government itself that violates the constitution and laws but because they are the top of the government, they ignore the laws and illegally* *act however they want without accountability. I think the police do the best they can but there are so many variables it is difficult to say unless a statistical analysis could be done to break it all down. I do feel this situation is so politically motivated that traditional law enforcement has had a great deal of difficulty doing a good job when government turns a blind eye to so many situations. I like guns but carrying them for safety depends on the situations. I can carry a gun in the woods for safety from bear and mountain lions, but I am guessing your talking in populated cities and suburbs. That is a tough question to answer and can't offer an opinion other than the dangerous people are the criminals that carry guns. I think the main causes for increased crime in America is the liberal administration that has an agenda to destroy our country and what it used to be.*

*Cynthia: "1. Is crime a serious problem where you live? City, town, or state?*

*2. Do the police do a good job in your country? I do not have much interaction with them.*

*3. Is carrying a gun a good way to stay safe? Why or why not? Yes. It is a necessary weapon for stopping harm against one's self of one's loved ones.*

*4. Do you think the world will be safer or more dangerous in the future? Dangerous*

*5. What were the main causes for our increase in crime across America? Lack of morality and removal of boundaries with consequences*

*David: "Crime is running rampant in America and as the election has shown people are perfectly happy to accept this by the way they voted, Illinois for example with all that is going there in Chicago, it didn't seem to matter to the population, same in New York, Detroit, and other cities, so the next time someone gets killed you can thank to people who voted for it! In some areas of America, they are doing a great job in spite of the people hating them in other areas I wouldn't risk my life for people who spit on you, they reap what they sow, America as it is today it's a good idea to carry a gun because in plain English it ain't safe anymore!"*

*Linda: "I live in the Black Hills of SD and although crime is not a problem at all here, it is, in the largest city near me. It has gotten worse in the last 2 years since the current Democrat turned Socialist administration took over.*

*Our police force does do a good job, but they are understaffed but most South Dakotans "back the Blue". We have many people moving here from CA and other Blue States and I venture to opine that they bring their trouble with them, although they are trying to escape the very thing, they bring with them. We are a RED State and welcome all.... but I think that is where we are wrong.*

*We have open and concealed carry here, no certification needed, and most of us do carry. Crimes with guns are by people who have obtained them illegally. And that proves that banning firearms will never work......criminals who cannot have them will always find a way to get them.*

*I fear for my grandchildren's future because I believe it will get worse and especially so due to our current administration running this Country....it is being brought to her knees, so to speak. And I believe they are doing this on purpose, it is their plan.*

*The Socialist Left is ruining our Country. We need to secure our borders, especially the Southern border to stop the flood of illegal immigrants, many of whom are criminals. Human trafficking, drugs and crimes in general have flooded this great Nation of ours. And the expense of this is a huge burden on the Taxpayers. And yes; carrying a gun is a good idea because it is a necessity. Governor Kristi Noem is a great Governor and a Godsend to South Dakota. She did not feed into the COVID nonsense and kept South Dakota open. And despite what DeSantis claims, Kristi Noem was THE first Governor to do so. Our economy flourished; unemployment was very low. Kristi Noem left the decision to close businesses and schools up to the individuals, as it should be. We had a great 2 years during the plandemic and welcomed all from other States and Countries who wanted, for a short time perhaps, to feel FREE!!!!!*

*I pray for our great Country every day. And it is crystal clear to me what this current Socialist agenda administration has done and continues to do. Other Countries laugh at us and see us growing weaker. They SEE that crimes of the Left go unpunished. They SEE the vote rigging......the only way we have to fight against them. The Left wants Socialism, and we must fight them at every turn. So sad I have to teach my very young Grandchildren this.... but I do. They deserve to grow up in the America that I grew up in."*

**Cindi:** *"Crime is a problem. Our police are so so. Yes, carry a gun. With liberals in charge the world will get worse*

**Teresa:** *I'm in a small rural area. Crime isn't a huge issue. The police here are wonderful. I fully support the second amendment for self-protection. Everyone should be prepared at all times to protect you or your family. I think our future is looking scary with a huge increase in crime. I feel the reason for this is society lowering its moral standards and not choosing to live in a Christlike manner. Without God* *nothing can prosper."*

***Candy:*** *"I live in a small-ish but growing town in Oklahoma! Crime is high in our larger cities here but nothing like New Yuck and Commiefornia!! The police in my state do a great job!! They make arrests and our DAs here are not Soros paid prosecutors!! They are real, by the book DAs!! Crime has increased because of Democrat leadership!! They have constantly called for defunding police, and they are the ones who pushed for cashless bail so the criminals could get right back out and commit more crimes or murder more innocent people!! EVERYWHERE there is a demoKKKrat running a city or state, there is VERY high crime and murder!!"*

***Carl:*** *"It's awful. They have watered down the juvenile laws to a point where there are zero consequences. Car theft, larceny, shootings. No consequences. Liberal CT."*

***Robert:*** *"A few weeks ago, in my city three officers were gunned down with two fatally wounded. The state of Connecticut is all in on prison and bail "reform" Safer? I would say NOT"*

***Jack:*** *"Carry Steel Peace of mind wherever I go. Even N.H. is no longer safe."*

***Lola:*** *"The death of George Floyd and others at the hands of police has diminished trust and provoked anger against police. A few rotten apples have cast a dark shadow on all police diminishing trust. That trust will take work to rebuild. They are taking steps to do that."*

***Anonymous:*** *"1. Crime in our city. Very small town (Wal Mart is the biggest thing we have), but lots of industry in the area and still growing. Nothing huge, but plenty of catalytic converter thefts, shoplifting, domestic violence, child abuses (to the point of deaths), assaults, fights, drugs, break ins, and shootings that seem to be increasing (murders that seem to be happening monthly or even more) Much more crime than when we came here (about 15 years). Our state seems to have major problems in the large cities. Drugs and murders seem commonplace. But that has been the case for many years in the big cities. the numbers are just increasing. BUT this type of crime is person to person, private disputes getting out of hand. The drive by shootings, though is an issue as it gets innocents. However, the one-on-one situations truly do not bother me much. Both parties are normally guilty, and both usually deserve what they get.*

*2 .The police patrol frequently. They are very visible, but IMHO, they do little. Assaults that have been reported and witnessed are NOT pursued by the police. They "look into it" for months and do nothing. It seems to matter WHO the perp is. Newcomer victims (those not native to the area) will pretty well be brushed off. Even when the problem people have long history of issues. Police in the schools manage to be away from wherever the problem is happening. One or two officers in a school that is spread out everywhere are as good as useless. And in the schools that would be considered safer (the younger children), they are almost useless. They are decorative and often are NOT there except for an occasional pass thru or drive by. They spend more time flirting with the staff than patrolling. Securing ALL entrances to the schools is more effective than police. When they are called, their response time is pathetically slow.*

*3. I am pro-gun. That said, when the idiots and hot heads are armed, it causes more problems than it helps. I would have no problem with knowing that convenience stores were armed. But as a whole, these bozos have little knowledge or INTEREST in SAFE gun handling. AND the automatic type weapons have no real use other than mass destruction. Armed IDIOTS are dangerous.*

*4. I believe the world (or our nation) will become less safe. The downsizing of the police, and the lack of ENFORCING laws (EVEN or ESPECIALLY when the disregard of the laws - the Constitution_ stats at the TOP LEVEL) does nothing to help or protect us. The examples of the riots and burnings, looting that has happened and nothing done is a prime example. Lawlessness ignored! As there is no punishment for the wrongdoing, more and more people will take matters into their own hands. This is NOT SAFE, but when no help is given, it will become necessary. Again, lack of enforcing the law by the police and the courts will drive us to this.*

*5. The causes are many. Recently, the lack of consequences (enforcement) is the main reason. WHY NOT? NOTHING WILL HAPPEN TO ME!) This BEGINS at the home, and in the schools. The lack of discipline and RESPECT in both places teaches the young that they have no rules. Poverty or GREED. Poverty because they do not GET JOBS. They have few skills because they did not bother to LEARN while they were in schools. The welfare system gives them funds, food, housing, medical care, phones. Even if they don't get those things, they LIVE WITH someone that gets those things for their children, and they live off those people. Kids do without so the deadbeats can live off things meant for the children. Drugs, selling and using cause many problems. The ease of getting drugs and the newer dangerous drugs pushes the crime higher. Greed. Always taking the easy way out. Why work to buy things? Just take them from those that DID work to earn things. Who or what will stop them? No punishment when they are caught. Whenever possible take the easy way out. Lie and Steal. And this ALSO starts at the TOP LEVELS. With those that are IMMUNE to prosecution or sanctions or consequences."*

We wished that this individual would let us use his name, but he requested to remain anonymous, so we respect his wishes. We want to talk about question five when talking about the root problems of why there is crime in the first place. This person hit the nail right on the head. The lack of respect by our younger generation is way out of control. Respect starts in the home and when parents don't demand respect these kids feel they can do whatever they want. Next, they will mention poverty and jobs telling us people don't get jobs. That's another root cause of crime. Since COVID-19 hit in 2019, the federal government shut down the economy. With that, millions of jobs were lost, and people started going into poverty. We were suffering at the hands of politicians. However, in the Black community, it was even worse. With those already struggling with jobs in each community and being told by democrats they would help them; nothing came to fruition. Another issue was being on government benefits and believing the government would help the Black community. With no help and no jobs in a local community, people need to survive and do what they need to do to make sure their families get food to eat. At that point, it becomes survival mode, and everyone will do what they feel they need to do to survive. This happens in every community under the poverty line in respective states. We will get into the drug issue in another chapter. The last part we want to mention is what he said about no punishment being given to people who commit crimes. It's become laughable. We mentioned district attorneys who refuse to do their jobs to prosecute criminals; that is a huge part of soaring crime. Let's look at a few more comments.

*Terry:* *"Everything boils down to corruption. Law enforcement has high rate of corruption. Politicians even higher. Main cause of crime is greed. Money buys crime, plain and simple."*

We appreciate Terry's opinion, but we had to look up statistics to find out just how corrupt law enforcement officers are. We get it, some people just don't like the police and might say anything negative about policing. We looked up the Police Corruption Perceptions Index and here is what we found. "The purpose of the Police Corruption Perceptions Index is to provide a subjective measure of the level of corruption in a given country as perceived by its inhabitants." The United Police force, across this great nation, stands at an average of 4.68. Considering other countries like Mexico on our southern border stand at an average of 7.97 and Puerto Rico whose average is 6.93. We say police corruption is not as bad as they say; in fact, better than most nations throughout this world.

*Larry:* "*Petty theft is common in my area. Murder and other such more serious crimes are far more common in other areas of town, as is the case in all poorly managed major population centers.*

*LEO performance varies but is less than satisfactory, for reasons mostly outside the control of individual officers or even their agencies — e.g., political interference*, inadequate finances for pre-employment screening and for adequate staffing levels, training, re-training, and even more retraining (to prepare officers for specific circumstances).*

*Responsible concealed or even open carry can have a deterrence effect, in addition to any safety provided.*

*Without sweeping improvements in public policies, crime will continue to increase.*

*Crime has increased because we have lost the deterrent effect of swift, certain, and (proportionately) severe punishment. Punishments are extremely delayed (by endless appeals, even when guilt is clear), uncertain (ridiculously variable from case to case and from jurisdiction to jurisdiction), and laughably lenient (e.g., 7 years for 1st degree murder).*

*Far more attention is given to protecting the "rights" of perpetrators than to protecting the legitimate rights of victims and potential future victims.*"

*Dennis:* "*In my city of Akron Ohio, we have a woke mayor who sides with social justice activists, so as a result criminals being arrested are bonded out right back on to the streets to commit more crimes. The police are trying to do their jobs despite the mayor really not having their backs. Yes, I do believe that carrying a gun is a good way to stay safe. Especially nowadays. I being you should properly trained to use one also. Things are definitely are going to get worse in the future. Look at the political climate. I believe the bible in what it says about Jesus coming back to take His true followers out of here and the earth being taken over by Satan. Just for a little while until God rains down His ultimate judgment upon the earth and Satan. The main increase if crime across America is people being influenced by Satan. Police are being handcuffed by their own city mayors who are afraid to take a stand against crime. Police Departments being defunded which leads to less officers on the streets. There are some bad apples in the bunch, but the majority of officers are doing their best to keep us safe. Anytime I can I go up to an officer to shake his or her hand to thank them for what they are doing."*

**Roger:** *"I contribute some of the crime wave to COVID. People laid off, no income, kids with boredom. COVID issues have gone away. There are enough jobs for anyone who wants to work and has the ability. Another issue is lack of parental involvement, and lack of community programs. Teens used to steal cars to sell to chop shops. Now they steal and abandon because it's something they saw on Tik Tok. Where are the parents in this? What programs are available to make kids feel a part of something, besides joining a gang? Are the programs and educational resources of equal quality and availability across all ethnicities and income levels? There is a lot of truth to the saying that "it takes a village to raise a child". Everyone watched us, parents, grandparents, neighbors, teachers; you didn't dare get out of line. You had chores, and were taught values, morality, responsibility, and respect. Somebody knew where you were and what you were doing at all times. Okay, I'm old, but I think we need more of that and less cell phone, free time, and hanging with friends."*

**Joseph:** *"Living in/near/around a metropolitan area since 1977. Crime has definitely become a serious issue. And I do believe the majority of the crime is drug related in one form or another. The root cause has many prongs to it and not enough resources are being used to lessen the increase."*

**Ralph:** *"1. Crime is not a problem until it visits you. I have lived near Detroit my entire life but keep moving further away. I am fearful to travel into the city because I have been robbed there.*

*2. Do the police do a good job in your country? Locally where I live now in a rural county police don't have much to do other than traffic tickets and domestic abuse. I guess that's a good thing, just make sure to slow down when entering town.*

*3. Carrying if trained properly is certainly beneficial.*

*4. "The World"? I read a stat in a book called Seven Tipping Points". I'll let it speak for itself "The best estimates of how many people that have ever lived on earth are about 100 to 110 billion. Fewer than 5 billion of earths inhabitants have ever lived under conditions that we consider free. That is about 4.5% of people who have ever lived."*

*5. What were the main causes for our increase in crime across America?  This one is more challenging but my opinion is there isn't enough male role models for young men. Men are broken, look around you, watch the news. Smash and grabs, looting stores, pushing people in front of trains, stomping on heads, beat downs on the subway, petty theft, homicides are up all over. There is a complete lack of respect for human life and disrespect for police. —70% of black children and 40% overall live in single parent homes. No Father around—Lack of male teachers means fewer male role models—Lack of church attendance means fewer male youth pastors Where do young men find their role models? The streets, movies, videos."*

*__Jerry:__ "1. Crime is not a serious problem where I live. But in California overall in 2021, homicides were up 47.2% and aggravated assaults were up 18%.*

*2. Police do a good job when they aren't hamstrung by politicians.*

*3. Yes, carrying a gun is a good way to stay safe. Because you shouldn't bring a wallet to a gunfight."*

We agree with Jerry that carrying a weapon is a great way to keep you and your family safe, as well as the community, should an active shooter situation occur near you. Unfortunately, the right to bear arms is the most complicated right we have today out of all our rights guaranteed by the constitution. It shouldn't be that way because a right is a right, period. These District Attorneys and politicians know that if you are not carrying a legal weapon but have one on you, automatically you are breaking the law. Just like illegal immigrants crossing the border. They know and we know they are here illegally, so they must be deported back to the homes, period.

*"4. If the global economy is good, crime will be lessened. And the obverse.*

*5. Don't know. Violent crime spiked higher when COVID hit, but that's only correlation. In general, crime tends to increase when poverty increases."*

*__Nikolay:__ 5. What were the main causes for our increase in crime across America? Relentless assault on the police by the democrats, reducing sentencing and prosecution for crimes, vilifying police based on misrepresentative statistics, instilling in minds of population that we have a systemic racism, misrepresenting exception cases as common occurrences, COVID lockdowns affected people psychology, economy, high unemployment, and few others stemming from the above mentioned.*

Since our politicians want to talk about crime in America, let's talk about this percentage. As of 2021, we have a population of approximately 332 million citizens living in the United States.

Currently, there are approximately 2 million inmates in prisons, and correctional facilities, the percentage point for that is less than 0.10 percent. We don't have a jail problem, we have a poverty problem and the failure of the Federal Department of Education, which is not a constitutional responsibility. Education is a state issue as well as what parents want to be taught in school. We do know this, if we worked for a major corporation and it kept failing its directors, people would lose their jobs. We the people have let this government get out of control. We need to create jobs and opportunities for all people and that will help to reduce crime in our neighborhoods. We will end with a quote that leads us in our next chapter. Keep on reading friends, we're almost finished.

**Cindi:** *"Increase in crime…. open borders, cashless bail, wok-ism, and people too lazy to work, who want a socialist country."*

# Chapter 9

# Open Borders and Immigration

Tell me how you feel about our immigration system today.

Tell me about your feelings on a border fence—does it slow down the influx of migrants, or should the U.S. make attempts to annex Mexico as part of the United States?

Should securing the border be the responsibility of each State or federal government and why? Or should both have that responsibility in protecting citizens?

Make any comments on immigration that you feel would benefit this conversation.

To answer these above questions let us start at the beginning of the forming of our country and an important document written by our forefathers, and that is the United States Constitution. Maybe we can get a few answers there on what responsibilities our federal government has to the citizens of this great country. This brings us to Article I Section 8 which states what the federal government responsibilities are. Two sentences that we will point out are the following: "To establish an uniform Rule of Naturalization, and uniform Laws on the subject of Bankruptcies throughout the United States."

"Article I, Section 8, Clause 4 of the Constitution provides Congress with the power . . . To establish an uniform Rule of Naturalization . . .throughout the United States.[1] The Supreme Court has described naturalization as the act of adopting a foreigner, and clothing him with the privileges of a native citizen.[2] Pursuant to this authority, Congress may legislate terms and conditions by which a foreign-born national (alien) may become a U.S. citizen.[3] Moreover, Congress's power over naturalization is exclusive; states may not impose their own terms and conditions by which aliens may become U.S. citizens.[4] Based on this broad power, Congress has enacted a series of laws governing the naturalization of aliens in the United States since the end of the eighteenth century.[5] These naturalization laws have generally applied to three main categories of aliens: (1) those who have resided in the United States for certain periods of time and applied for naturalization; (2) those born abroad to U.S. citizen parents; and (3) those who derived citizenship after their parents naturalized in the United States.[6]

Congress's power under the Naturalization Clause is not limited to conferring citizenship. The Supreme Court has recognized the power as also giving Congress the ability to revoke citizenship improperly obtained through fraud or other unlawful means.[7] Additionally, the Court has recognized that Congress has the power to expatriate an individual who, through some voluntary act, has relinquished his or her U.S. citizenship.[8]

In addition to conferring Congress with power to determine when foreign nationals may obtain U.S. citizenship, the Naturalization Clause is sometimes viewed as contributing to Congress's power over immigration, including its power to set rules for when aliens may enter or remain in the United States. In those few paragraphs, the federal government has the authority to allow immigrants to enter our country. Nowhere does it say we must let illegal immigrants enter since we have laws to follow for migrants to enter the United States of America. The government is failing the citizens of this country. There is more in the constitution we want to show under the same Article I Section 8, specifically this clause; "To provide for calling forth the Militia to execute the Laws of the Union, suppress Insurrections and repel Invasions." There is no doubt in our minds that the Biden administration has caused an invasion on our southern borders. Since becoming president, approximately four million illegal aliens have crossed into our country. There are approximately another million that crossed without detection. How can this country afford to care for another six million people? We can't take care of United States citizens but will spend money to help illegal immigrants. Doesn't seem fair to Americans that presidential administrations help every country out there but leave their own citizens behind. All politicians today have failed the American first initiative, which is keeping citizens safe in our country. Jack stated, "In my lifetime this immigration problem started in the 1980s which is also when America started forgetting about the fourth check on government, the constituents. Then, as the decades went by and the same hacks stayed in office, they discovered another subject to divide the people who pay them, which is immigration. Now we have nothing but crooked politicians on both sides of the aisle who use news media outlets to tell us we are wrong about immigration. Since when do residents who live on the border have no rights as American citizens? And it's spreading across this country. This is an insult to all of us and it is every politician's way to divide us even more than they have."

The constitution is an amazing document that has stood the test of time. Not only in Article I Section 8, but there is also another Amendment that tells the government about its duty to protect we the people. The reason why we put the U.S. Constitution in this book was not only to get people to read it but to also reference it when needed. Article 4 Section 4 states, "The United States shall guarantee to every State in this Union a Republican Form of Government and shall protect each of them against Invasion; and on Application of the Legislature, or of the Executive (when the Legislature cannot be convened) against domestic Violence." Of course, these politicians that we have elected today will only tell you one version of what invasion is and to them, it's "an occasion when an army or country uses force to enter and take control of another country." They honestly believe that we the people are stupid and that is the only way they can protect American citizens. However, there are other definitions of what invasion is, which they fail to mention to us. Here are two more definitions, the first is, "an occasion when a large number of people or things comes to a place in an annoying and unwanted way" and second, "an occasion or process that affects someone's life in an unpleasant and unwanted way." We really don't believe that the home and landowners, especially in Texas, wanted migrants to come on their land and be part of their lives. That is how stupid our government is when dealing with immigrants. We believe, for most of us living here, we want legal migrants to enter this country and become legal citizens of the United States. What we don't want are illegal immigrants just crossing the border because the president says it is all right, those are unwanted immigrants. The federal government is not the only villain here, we also must blame it on border states like Nevada, Arizona, and Texas, for each state is sovereign and has the right to protect its citizens. States can't rely on the federal government for everything, especially their incapability to secure the border.

When we look at the Constitution of Texas under Article I "Bill of Rights" under Section 1 it states, "Texas is a free and independent State, subject only to the Constitution of the United States, and the maintenance of our free institutions and the perpetuity of the Union depend upon the preservation of the right of local self-government, unimpaired to all the States. (Feb. 15,

1876.)" That tells us that although they need to follow the U.S. Constitution, they are free to create their own laws to protect their own citizens—just as other states have the same powers to protect the people in their respective states. If you look at the Texas Constitution, Article IV Section 7 reads, "**GOVERNOR AS COMMANDER-IN-CHIEF OF MILITARY FORCES.** He shall be Commander-in-Chief of the military forces of the State, except when they are called into actual service of the United States. He shall have power to call forth the militia to execute the laws of the State, to suppress insurrections, and to repel invasions. (Feb. 15, 1876. Amended Nov. 2, 1999.) (Temporary transition provisions for Sec. 7: see Appendix, Note 1.)"

Just like the federal constitution, this state constitution has the authority to stop invasions. Not just put them on buses and send them to New York, Washington, D.C., and Chicago. However, in our opinion these border states want to blame everything on the federal government. It's their answer for not securing the border. That is what these states want people to believe, but securing the border is a dual responsibility between the federal and state government. Each citizen must hold federal and state politicians accountable for securing the border, because this issue affects us the most. Our politicians could care less if an illegal immigrant comes on your land, shoots you or a family member, or if drug cartels distribute drugs on your land. Just don't send them to Martha's Vineyard; that is when they get annoyed.

The drug epidemic in this country has reached crisis levels. The number of individuals who overdose yearly has almost reached one million people. That is a major problem that politicians refuse to resolve or fail to resolve. Fentanyl kills more than half of opioid users which equals 53%. In 2020, more than 42,000 people died from fentanyl. Most of these illegal drugs come from the drug cartels in Mexico. They are the leading supply chain of all illegal major drugs in the United States. That is cocaine, heroin, and methamphetamines. Our government gives Mexico billions of dollars in assistance to help fight these cartels, but that gets us nowhere. We have more major crime in this country than we have had at any time in our history. Yes folks, open borders fuel our drug epidemic right here in the United States of America. Where are our politicians at with everything going on with the border? No one seems to want to fix it. The Governor of Texas, Greg Abbott, has been busing migrants to Washington, D.C. for a few months.

Now Arizona is doing the same thing and it's starting to put a strain on D.C. resources. I have heard more than six thousand migrants have volunteered to go to D.C. and now politicians are getting upset. Some are now concerned about receiving migrants when they remained silent since Biden started his open border policy. "Well, this is a very significant issue. We have for sure called on the federal government to work across state lines to prevent people from really being tricked into getting on buses. We think they're largely asylum seekers who are going to final destinations that are not Washington, D.C. I worked with the White House to make sure that FEMA provided a grant to a local organization that is providing services to folks. I fear that they're being tricked into nationwide bus trips when their final destinations are places all over the United States of America," said the Mayor of Washington, D.C. That shows everyone right there that these political parties won't work together to resolve an important issue that the American people want solved. This is the nonsense that each of us must listen to daily on our fake news networks. The republicans throw the same misinformation out there and people are brainwashed by these parties, it's sad. People need to work together on both sides of the aisle to solve these issues we are talking about in this chapter and the ones you have already read. Let's see what some people across the country had to say about the three questions listed above.

*__Thorstein:__ "1. Immigration policies today do not make sense. It is about stopping the bleeding. It is going to get much worse in the next 100 years. If you seriously believe in stopping immigration, you need to stop the cause of bleeding. Why do people come here? If people do not want to come here, you have no problem. Persecution has always been the reason people seek the USA since its foundation. In the 1800's it was "Give us your..."Now it is "NO!!!"*

*A wall is not going to work; more police help a bit but sending them to democrats is a cop-out. Truth also is the USA population is stable with present immigration and will shrink without immigration. So, the question is who and how many do we accept, not secure the border (which again is not a solution, too many come via other ways). Another thought. Immigration has always benefited the USA. Immigrants fight harder for the USA; they pay more taxes and promote stability and take low jobs. Global warming is the future immigration wave. Already the equator is becoming uninhabitable. Doorknobs are so hot people wear gloves to open doors. etc. They will want to move to better climates. The USA has a lot of unoccupied acreage. It will be seen for this. People under the present rules of tyranny will continue to see the USA as the best choice. You think holding the growing wave is hard now? it could become a wave like the Starship Troopers movie.*

*This has never honestly been a political party issue. The present admin and each prior one for 50 years struggled with this issue. THE SOLUTION IS RIGHT IN FRONT OF YOU. The best result has always been to help make people happy to stay where they are."*

***Jessi:*** *"Hi Dennis. My thoughts on this are so deeply entangled with an over-all theory of how we need to handle the division of State and Federal power and responsibilities overall, to prevent us from ever having these vile treasonous cowards have the power to put our country in peril ever again, so it is a little complicated, but I hope the following helps. Have a great Thanksgiving.*

*1. Our current system for dealing with immigration is purposely broken and being used to help destroy our country. People that come here legally, for example my husband, from England, have to pay thousands and jump through many hoops, but I always felt that the process was designed to vet immigrants to prevent criminals from invading our Country. It was very stressful for us, but the current administration has actively encouraged illegal immigrants to pour into our country, un-documented, un-vetted.*

*2. The wall was part of the solution. President Trump also leveraged the aid that we pay to Mexico and other Latin American Countries, to force them to take their people back and had the Mexican Military helping secure our borders. We should not annex parts of Mexico; this would only lead to war.*

*3. States should have the ultimate responsibility to secure our borders, but the Feds should support them in their endeavors to enforce our laws. As a matter of fact, the Federal government should be limited to acting as our representatives on the world stage, coordination of military action if the states decide that we need to deploy our military, they should no longer collect and manage taxes, Social Security and Medicare as we know it should be disbanded and the states, under instruction of the local precincts should contribute to the salaries of the Federal government based on a new, reasonable salary guidelines.... but this is off topic. ☺ The gist is taken away all power except the judiciary, from the feds.*

*4. Legal immigration can enhance our society, but it must be controlled. Illegal immigration is a burden on the taxpayers, a threat to the safety of those in border states, and beyond as the illegals spread out."*

***Thomas:*** *"Still waiting on Mexico to cut a check for Donnie Bone Spurs border wall."*

***Bryan:*** *1. Like everything else in the US, it exists. It could be better, and I am an offspring of immigrants. I'm no more native to this country than another who isn't a direct descendant of a Native American.*

*2. There are lots of oceans that could be used if the border was walled off. It's a nationalist idea at best and racist at its worst. People want to be here for a reason, they will get in if needed.*

*3. Obviously a federal issue. Again, unless you are a Native American, people should be empathetic towards those who see this as a country that is better than their current country.*

*4. This is a country that was not discovered by ANYONE of European decent. Compassion and empathy go a long way in this world.*

*PS- This isn't a soap box stand for open borders. Please, understand this is a country of immigrants, always has been (following herds of animals) always will be."*

***Lisa:*** *1. I think the system needs to be tweaked. Vet the ones coming in legally faster. Get them working faster. No reason it should take them so long to be able to work.*

*2. a fence helps control who is coming in. But we have to fix our system to get them in faster. But illegally is the best way to let the bad ones in.*

*3. mostly federal should take care of it.*

***Ronald:*** *"That's a simple one.*

*1. The immigration system is broken. Look at what is happening in the south and north. They are coming from both directions.*

*2. Border walls are a must. Yes, it may not stop but it slows down the influx issue. Look almost every Senator and Congress live in GATED communities so if it's good for them.*

*3. Both should take responsibility, but the Federal Government should pay most if not all it is one Country."*

***Yusif:*** *"Our immigration system should accommodate migrant workers. The border fence is a lot of nonsense. Protecting our borders must be a federal responsibility, and no we shouldn't try to annex Mexico!*

***Theresa:*** *1. not enforcing border crossing legal policy. Allowing them to come across and moving them all over the U.S.*

*2. The fence would not keep them all out but would definitely slow it way down and allow more to be caught that climb it.*

*3. When federal government does not do their job the states should have the right to step in protect its borders and send the bill to the federal government to be paid.*

***Tim:*** *"The border starts with your home, neighborhood, town, county, state, country. In that order. Each is responsible for their domain. No, we do not need to annex Mexico, we need to destroy the drug cartels."*

In question #2 we also asked if the United States should annex Mexico and become part of this country. A few individuals above said no to that idea, and we can respect their views. Annexing Mexico may be a smarter move that could benefit American citizens and Mexican citizens. Here's why we feel that way. Illegal immigrants come to America for several reasons, especially a better way of life. They look for better-paying jobs, and safer communities for their children to grow up in. They dream just like we do, but it comes at a cost for them to come here to America. If we were to annex Mexico as part of the USA, all sorts of business owners would open operations there, putting millions of their people to work. They would not have to leave to get a better way of life since they could build it right there. They could start building new, safer communities. That would also generate more tax revenue from business which would directly help all citizens. Here are two numbers that most people don't research and that is that Mexico has 132 million citizens living there, and the United States has approximately 37 million Mexican people living here, just over ten million are illegal migrants. That brings us to our next point. Mexico is about three times larger than the state of Texas. Adding 100 million citizens to our country will grow the tax base over thirty percent. Mexican citizens are hardworking, family-orientated people who want to see their children succeed. That's part of why they migrate to the United States. If annexed, all money in Mexico would become part of U.S. revenue. So, before we say no to annexation, we need to research the benefits for both countries. It seems to work out in our favor, plus it would stop illegal immigration.

Another point to make that  should be looked at by our politicians in conjunction with the government of Mexico is that we share approximately 2,000 miles along the southern border. That is a lot of ground to cover to look for illegal immigrants. Mexico also shares a border with Guatemala and Belize and shares Maritime ports with Cuba and Honduras, 540 miles with Guatemala and 160 miles with Belize, which averages 700 miles of a border that would need to be secured. Let us do some math here and see what we come up with. That's almost 2,000 miles on the Southern border that immigration and customs border patrol must try to secure daily. They don't have the resources to cover that much territory. However, if we annexed Mexico and secured the border with Guatemala and Belize, which is 700 miles, we would have a much safer and secure country. We would be able to move our resources down to that border and our federal enforcement officers would be able to do a better job of keeping the American people safe. This would also add the element of saving human life at our southern border. Many migrants end up dying trying to cross the desert and across the Rio Grande. We could stop people from dying—how great would that be? We can limit human trafficking by these drug cartels. There would be no need to try and get here illegally, because now they are United States Citizens.

We won't get into how their natural resources could help our country. You can read on and see what others had to say about this issue.

*Virginia:* *"Chucky Schumer said we need immigration because American women are not having children and we need the population increase. At the same time, they are saying we are overpopulated and have encouraged the women to have abortions. Pelosi said we need them to fill jobs that Americans won't do. But there are many Americans looking for work. These people coming into the country will not carry on the American values and the love for our country. This is a way the Dem's are destroying the country from within. In 10 yrs. or less we won't be celebrating Thanksgiving or Christmas because that doesn't mean anything to the immigrants, they will celebrate their holidays and traditions. How did we get to where our own government hates its people and chooses other countries and people over Americans. Hold on American's love your country doesn't lose faith. We are #America Strong. We can be great again. God bless America. PRAY."*

*Scott:* *"The policy's we have aren't enforced. The fence should be completed. It will stop or slow illegal immigration and drug smuggling across OUR southern border. It's the responsibility of our federal government to secure our nation and its citizens.*

*The Wall should be constructed with federal first then state participation. Legal immigration is part of our founding and history. LEGA."*

**Jim:** *"#1 The sociological impact from the high levels of immigrants crossing the borders by sea or land is only going to slow down when our policies discourage financial incentives. The taxpayer funded system is here to make sure that it encourages legal immigration on the path to citizenship.*

*#2 As much as physical obstacles can be a deterrence for illegal immigrants crossing, it shouldn't be confused with a comprehensive or effective solution when the states are approached by land or sea. The immigration process should resolve the matter by the design of legal immigration standards determined and funded by a combination of state and federal government agencies. Should we annex another country with a narco economy that our poorly established class 1 drug categories are shaped by pharmaceutical monopolies that create the black market from these prohibitions. I would choose Legalization and free drug treatment programs before annexation of any narco economy that would otherwise Dissolve without black market conditions that created it.*

*#3 Both should pay; federal policy directly impacts the amount of immigration a state must deal with. If you don't have a seat at the table, you are what's for dinner."*

**Mark:** *"Immigration... I live in Uvalde Texas. We have dealt with an influx of invaders since February 2021. The schools took no issue with lock downs last May, due to getting lock downs almost twice a week since February 2021 from IA's evading law enforcement in a vehicle. Our property, livelihoods, and costs to repair our properties is substantial. Our lives, our children's lives, and neighbors have been hurt substantially. Crazy issue is when these IA's get sent to NY and the Hamptons, they want a to issue a National Emergency! What about the citizens living in the FEBA (forward edge of the battle area)?"*

**Bert:** *"It is obviously needing improvement. What we need is a faster processing system. Immigration has been and is a major positive for this nation's economy. There is far too much fear mongering among the pundits and politicians. That being said it isn't fair for the border states to take on the full burden of the influx. Especially with a system that forces these people to hide from registering and participating with the system. A huge problem with the border wall discussion is and was Trump. He went in projecting racist tropes in his calls for a border wall. That naturally created a negative reaction to the concept of border walls. Some walls make a lot of sense and can help with processing. It was never realistic to create a complete wall across the* *southern border and (like every other program) would be something like 10 times the costs that were being proposed to achieve it. Denial of this is just biased wishful thinking. Expansion and true enforcement of E-verify or an upgraded version seems the most logical. However again efficiency of processing must be a primary focus. The important thing is to identify and keep track of these immigrants. The vast majority come in order to work. Hard working people are never bad for an economy. Creating a fear-based system of deportation turbo charges the black market, provides drug mules, is bad for our economy and is in-humane and unethical. Making alcohol illegal didn't work and created all kinds of crime and social issues. Same thing is happening with this. Then the pundits claim these people are criminals just like they claimed those who drank alcohol were criminals. Sometimes the problem isn't the people sometimes it's the stupid law. Simply create a system of rules, that these people must follow associated with working and paying taxes and reporting and put the resources into monitoring and tracking and deport those who come and fail to comply to a system setup so they can easily comply. If they don't have to fear and know they can participate they will for the vast majority register and keep up with reporting so they can continue to participate. It's not rocket science."*

**Carolyn:** *"All our tax money will be used to support these people. I want tax dollars to support America's poor and help kids who need private tutoring".*

**Monica:** *"First of all…we should have a border wall. Every single politician has used the border issues as a talking point to get elected or reelected. Going back for decades. This isn't a new problem. The issue and the solutions should be a collaboration from both states and federal officials. One issue that needs to be addressed is our lawmakers profiting off of an open border. Not all migrants are bad. However, if they choose to come across the river rather than a point of entry…it makes them a criminal. Which shows they have zero respect for American laws. The staggering amount of drugs being brought through our borders is a danger to citizens in all 50 states. There isn't even 1 city in America that hasn't been touched or effected by the drugs. Which comes back to the profits of it. There is big money in the drug business on the side of the cartels and local, state, federal governments. The fact that they are killing American citizens, ruining families, and destroying communities makes no difference to them as they make a lot of money off of the courts, probation, family services, adoption of children whose parents are addicted, CT. We also have people who are south of the border who are organizing large groups to come into our country in an effort to change regulation…which is an invasion. I don't believe state governors should be using*

*American tax dollars to ship these people to other states. But at the same time...these states have encouraged the invasion. And refuse to do anything to curb, slow, or stop it. So, something has to be done to start a conversation...people's lives depend on it. We spend so much taxpayer money on immigration, but we have soldiers who gave limbs and parts of their soles...some lost everything to protect our country and today a lot of them are sleeping in the streets while we prioritize illegals and immigrants over them. It's not right. We should take care of America first. Our safety and security should come before foreigners."*

*__Vince:__ "Immigration should be conducted legally. the wall should be built. have we forgotten 9/11? what's the purpose of homeland security? the drug cartels are loving the open border."*

*__Darwin:__ "There is a legal pathway to citizenship in this country that worked. The liberals have deliberately broken the system in order to gain power. Eventually this will collapse the system for everyone. And then America will end up looking like the country's that these immigrants are fleeing from. With the same kind of dictators and military rule that they wanted to get away from."*

*__Scott:__ "# 1My ex-wife I personally immigrated from Canada. The immigration process to the US isn't that difficult. But there is the time involved in it becoming a reality and there very well should be. For example, the most important item when we crossed from Canada into the US on her way in right before our marriage was her chest x-ray, and for a very good reason. Tuberculosis isn't a joke, and it runs rampant in 3rd world countries as they don't vaccinate for it. In Central America, during the global Covid outbreak more people died from tuberculosis than covid -19.*

*#2. A border fence is a must. We don't want open borders for 1 specific reason. We are fucking broke. All that jump the fence, per se aren't here to improve our economy as hard-working taxpaying citizens, they are coming for the welfare and to get a free lunch. Also, take into consideration that most crossing illegally are not very educated, and are not the cream of the crop. Mexico has many successful businessmen, and they have beautiful beaches but that alone isn't worth the burden of all the poverty to claim for the US.*

*#3. the Initial cost of fencing the border should be the federal government as that is the outer boundaries. The feds should then pay an annual per-mile cost for maintenance and security. It would easily be within budget if we kill the foreign aid policy and freeze the stupidity that gets funding by adding into a bill on the*

*floor of the house. Line-item veto would take care of that and the elimination of corrupted voting, so we get decent politicians that actually care about our country and not themselves.*

*#4. Look at the US immigration system in the late 1800s. You saw our ancestors lined up for seemingly never-ending lines to LEGALLY immigrate to America through Ellis Island. Most of the immigrants where I grew up came to America for an opportunity. They also knew enough that it was only capable through hard work, cultivating prairie land that had never been broken and making it all on their own. None of those immigrants had it easy as many didn't even speak English upon arrival. But they all learned it and knew it was 1 common ground to be a part of this country. But they all had 1 thing in common, they knew it wasn't going to be easy. but with hard work, it could be achieved. They never came here to be a burden to anyone, but instead, to help make America grow by earning their keep and making sure their children worked hard to get their chance to succeed and fulfill the American dream. When America entered both WW1 and WW2 it was many less than 50 years into being Americans who volunteered to the Armed Services because of how important this " Home of the Brave and land of the Free " is and that there is no other place in the world quite like it. The only way we can keep our country like that is by legal immigration for those willing to become an asset to our great land, not merely a leach to our society, as that part of our country is more than already maxed out, with the democratic party promoting it.*

**Leonard:** *"Immigration Might be good but in most cases it's always insecurities to the Countries Migrants are going to Coz;*

*(a) Most Migrants might be Robbers, Terrorists, Thieves and Gangsters Which might Harm the Nation in Future.*

*(b) Migrants might be Invade the Neighboring Country in a Very Large number which might put the Nation In to Future Poverty and Hunger.*

*(c) In Most Cases migrants always affect The National Government through Lack of Citizenship Opportunities and Leeds the nation to bribery....... Hence, every Nation Must have Perimeter Wall and Tight Security."*

**Tamara:** *"I have friends here from South Africa...they have to pay sometimes large sums of money for whatever the government decides...just to stay...all in the so-called application process...but yet...some of our states are handing out a life of ease and entitlement to illegals...they pay for nothing... The only thing some Americans* *have is citizenship to this beautiful, wonderful country…but now it seems like more of a downfall…"*

***Andrew:*** *"Our immigration system is completely broken. We've had the highest illegal immigration numbers in decades in the last 22 months. While the wall wasn't perfect, it definitely slowed it down to the lowest since 2009. As far as protecting our borders, it's the responsibility of the federal government, hence why we have CBP, a federal agency. The state bears some responsibility, but the feds are the ones mainly in charge of it. If the government refuses, as in this current administration, then the state has legal authority to secure the border by any and all legal means."*

***Scott:*** *"People don't realize that this country is being run into the ground on purpose…… the Invasion through our southern border benefits the democrats who offer a "better life" in exchange for votes. But that "better life" is nothing more than our welfare system which is designed to keep people dependent on the government. Our nation's best days are behind us. Our nation is no longer secure, and the only people to blame are ignorant voters."*

***Ted:*** *"First off…. reality lesson…. rich people are leading this country…. they are much smarter than average Americans. Rich people have changed the conversation regarding immigrants because they love the cheapest labor that the world can offer….and no border will stop or even slow their greed for low wage slaves. They have bought the 2 parties and 3rd parties to set the tone that anyone opposing an open border is a racist. That way most Americans will not challenge the wealthy people bringing so many into the country. In a nutshell…. yes, we have allowed in way too many immigrants in the last 30 years….it has driven wages for Americans down. Even immigrants in USA want the border closed…. now that they are here…. we grew by 100 million people in 40 years…. way to fast…. let's slow down…. give the immigrants here green cards but also secure the border and stop all immigration for a couple years!"*

Each one of these individuals who answered our questions had something of value to add to the discussion. These questions and comments as well as everything that we have said throughout this book have been our opinion. We all stand firm on what we have said. We will end this chapter with three quotes that should wake a few people up and think about illegal immigration. Please read on to the next chapter.

**Rita:** *"I'll reply to # l. What immigration system? There is none at all, under this "president" and one is desperately needed."*
**Don:** *"Complete failure"*
**Lester:** *"What immigration system, we have an open border."*

# Chapter 10

# "Racism in America"

Why is there so much racism in America today?

Why do politicians want to divide ethnic groups against each other?

It's unfortunate that we even need to mention this subject of racism in America today. It is a thorny subject that most people don't want to talk about. We will either be called racists for talking about this or people will open their eyes and see the real reason behind racial tensions in our country. In this day and age, we shouldn't even be talking about this, we thought this problem was dealt with several times. The first time this was addressed was right after the Civil War when this country came together and passed Amendment XIII which states: SECTION 1. "Neither slavery nor involuntary servitude, except as a punishment for crime whereof the party shall have been duly convicted, shall exist within the United States, or any place subject to their jurisdiction." Passed by Congress in January 1865 and ratified on December 6, 1865. This was the first time that citizens of this country united and said every person would be free, no matter their color. After that amendment was passed it seemed like the issue was never finally put to rest. We still had racism and when would it stop? There are always going to be racist people in this great country, we won't be able to stop it completely and that is a shame. There is no time for racism in America today, we have countries that want to do us harm, and the people that will be fighting for us will have no skin color. They will be the men and women of our United States Military. The only color they will see is green. The men and women who will support them will be called **PATRIOTS** and they will be male and female from every ethnic group in this country.

The topic of racism showed its ugly head again in the fifties and sixties. We had white and black people that were pure evil, white restaurants that kept black people out, and African Americans who were told they could only ride the back of a bus. How was that fair to paying customers? It wasn't, until a few people stood up and said, No more. Rosa Parks would not sit in the back any longer and she held her ground. Martin Luther King came out of nowhere and started uniting and showed up at certain places where white people were gathering and we all know his famous speech, "I have a Dream." He stood his ground and started changing the way people looked at color. We need more people like him and Rosa Parks to lead this country, black people, white people, Hispanic and Asian people who are tired of this race problem we have in America. By the way, maybe you should take a minute and listen to his speech, it may inspire you to get involved with stopping racial tensions.

Politics is the root of all evil, some say that money is, but we say it's politics. Politicians want to put their thumb on we the people and unfortunately, many citizens are brainwashed to the garbage they are being told by these elected officials. Racism is brought up daily in mainstream media news outlets who are only an extension of our two major political parties. Politicians totally understand that if they divide this country by race that they can control the narrative. In doing that they get you to believe that they are honest and caring and will fix your problems. When was the last time either the Republican or Democrat party helped the little people out? The little people we mean is you and I, the people who go to work hand in hand with people of other races and get along fine in their work environment daily. Most of us don't care about skin color, or religion or even your sexual preference. It is the politicians that have created this racism monstrosity, not we the people. We are the ones who must end this topic once and for all. We have had enough of hate in this country, we cannot be divided anymore. Once we are united these politicians will run scared, they have no control over a nation united.

We have already talked about the military and how all races come together to see only green, let us mention sports such as the National Football League. There are eleven players on offense and eleven on defense. The players on this field are black, white, Asian, and Hispanic, all races who must work together to stop the other team from advancing. They practice several days each week and come together once a week united. The only color they know is teammate. Maybe we can learn something with teamwork because together we all achieve more. There cannot be any I's, we can't be individuals, we must be part of the team, a bigger picture of winning back this country we have handed over to tyrants.

The democratic party tells us the republican party are racist and the people that believe in republican values also believe in racism. That could not be farther from the truth. Let us review a little history lesson of racism in politics. We already mentioned the Civil War and how slavery was abolished. The person who led that charge was Abraham Lincoln, a republican. Here are a few facts that most people don't know about. We will give you a quick refresher starting with West Virginia Senator Robert Byrd who served from 1952 until his death in 2010, the longest-serving Senator in political history. Here is what people don't know about this Senator. Prior to being elected to the Senate, Byrd was a high-ranking member of the Ku Klux Klan. He formed the West Virginia chapter for that organization. Just look up Senator Robert Byrd and the Ku Klux Klan by Robert Longley in ThoughtCo. It is right there in black and white for everyone to see. He was a democrat and a racist. Are you starting to paint a picture yet? Next, we want to mention our current president Joe Biden who in 1975 embraced segregation and opposed a federally mandated busing policy to end segregation in schools. Again, another white politician who opposed the advancement of colored people. Look at this article in the Washington Examiner by Alana Goodman called "Joe Biden embraced segregation in 1975, claiming it was a matter of "black pride." We will do one more and end with important legislation called the 1964 Civil Rights Act. Democrats who say they are the saviors for the black community failed the black community with the no votes. In the senate, twenty-one democrats voted against it which equals 78%. In the house, ninety-six democratic lawmakers voted no, which equals 74%. If the democrats were really a party for equality and fairness, every single one of those members should have voted yes. The democratic party puts on a front to make black voters believe they are the party for the people. This legislation would not have passed without Republican leadership. Research this material and look at it yourself, we can't make this up. We mean we probably could, but no one would believe us. Research Democrat/GOP Vote Tally on 1964 Civil Rights Act in the Wall Street Journal/Opinion. Again, right there in black and white for everyone to see and make their own opinion on that story. We want people to know that we believe, in our opinion, that both the democratic and republican parties have let the people of this country down. It is time we all stand united against the corruption and tyranny. We can and must be the ones who win back our country from these political hacks who have done nothing but divide the people of the United States of America. Let's read what some people of America had to say about this topic.

*Jim:* *"Yours is an important question. The answer is so complicated that it's hard to grasp from a cause & effect view. But addressing it is critical to democracy, to its preservation. What is scary is that it is pervasive, not isolated to a region. Further, it's present even among "evangelicals" and while not stated publicly, evidenced among many likely to profess their faith, contrary to their denials of racist views."*

*Efbe:* *"I believe the only racism is that being made up by the left to, as you say, divide and conquer the people. It all comes from fear, and they use it well."*

*Gavin:* *"Not sure there is more racism today as there was 50-60-70 years ago. It's just move visible today. It's also easier to speak out against and it's long-term ramifications are now being recognized." "We overcome racism by being completely honest about it. Which we continue to fail to do. We right the wrongs that have been committed. Politicians are just playing the cards in front of them, but they are human just like everyone else." "They play those cards because they want power. And we know the saying "Power corrupts and absolute power corrupts absolutely.""*

*Billie:* *"I do not believe racism in itself is as big a problem as the divisive government wants people to believe. I feel the majority of the people don't care about the color of a person as much as the character of the person. I don't feel like most people even think about this subject until others continue to try to shove it in everyone's face."*

*Anonymous:* *"If by racism, you're referring to blatant racism against white heterosexual males, and blacks against each other and other ethnic groups, and the Danes against the indigenous people from Greenland, and Australia against their own indigenous people, there is racism. But it's not institutional. If you believe that it is, please tell me which institution is racist. Universities are favoring many underprivileged people for admission to their schools to the exclusion of Asians and others that are more qualified. I've experienced some anti-American sentiment in travels around the world too. For anyone to think that we are all going to sit and hold hands and sing Kum bye yah, they are mistaken. We have come a hell of a long way from where we were even 20 years ago and, until recently with so many fomenting racism and throwing it in our faces they are trying to convince us that racism is worse than ever. I disagree."*

*Joanne:* *"There always has been racism in America"*

*Allison:* *"America is not a racist country. Marxists and communists (some happen to be politicians), certainly, use racism to divide and weaken. We overcome racism and division by banning CRT and calling out the hypocrisy and liars who state America is racist. I encourage you to study how China was divided in a similar manner and weakened and is suffering so much because of communism and look at the history of how they divided China. Better to write a book about the atrocities occurring at our southern border by the installed Biden regime."*

**David:** *"In my opinion you will never overcome racism as long as the democrats keep calling us the Maga folks everything but human, their strategy is to divide the party between Trump and DeSantis , so as to split the republicans in half and if the republicans fall for that then they will lose , so the leftist will continue with their hate filled rhetoric, right up to the last minute in the 24 race for the presidency, and we have people like Joy Reid who is so full of hatred for white people and especially for those who support Trump and any republican , you have the talk shows like the view, Stephen Colbert, Kimmel, and others who keep perpetuating racism among other things , jimmy Kimmel is one who is a total Hypocrite and crybaby , one of his gigs was on the man show , where they exploited women and he dressed up in black face pretty much his entire body to make fun of Carl Malone a pro basketball player nothing is ever mentioned about this , but he calls racist for those supporting Trump , his hatred for Trump and those who support him is there for all to see ! There are many celebrities who pushed the racism and hatred card and they will do it again when Trump becomes the nominee and he will be the nominee , I guess everyone remembers Robert DeNiro and his rant of cursing and hatred towards a man who wanted to make America great and his rant also insulted the Maga folks, I myself don't see what is wrong with that logo and don't understand why so many people become so invested in their hatred for I believe we are on right side of this political issue and truly think some of these people need psychological help , as long as they keep feeding fear there are those who will never see themselves as being wrong and will never stop , we as Americans or I should say Maga Americans are not racist and are very happy that Latinos and black Americans are finally seeing the corruption from the democrats and media , Hollywood etc, but it sure took a long time , as long as the democrats and media push this narrative of hate and racism it will take a long time to recover from the damage they have created in our America , last words crime in America has risen exponentially and it's not helping black and Latino communities or any community for that matter, we can only hope as time moves on that a change can take place .I believe most of all this was started by Obama and wife that is when I first heard of hatred for America by a president and First Lady."*

**John:** *"I do not think the Republican or libertarian or independent parties really tried to divide ethnic groups... I believe it is a purely Democratic Party playing to help them keep power and get votes."*

**Nancy:** *"There is No systemic racism in the US unless you count the war on whitey. Race is being used as a tool to divide."*

**Kay:** *"The only racism in the United States is the democratic people that have pushed this fake agenda Positioning one race against the other when both races love each Other. It is shameful what they have done to our country in the last 2 years, and they're not done with us yet."*

**Dan:** *"First, there *isn't* so much racism in America today as compared to the past. The reason why there is as much as there is, is because it is an easily exploitable political tool. The people "in charge" of the poor conditions in the inner cities and minority communities must create boogeyman to deflect the blame onto people other than themselves."*

**David:** *"Why is there so much racism? Whites and Blacks never take responsibility for their own actions. The term institutional racism has been introduced as a scare tactic. Just what is institutional racism? Stacey Abrams has never defined it and she has used it many times. Go watch an episode of "Godfather of Harlem." That would fit the definition of institutional racism, but have those actors stood up and sacrificed their hit EPIC series? No, they haven't. The Republicans selected a black candidate to counter Warnock. Is that not institutional racism? Draw that black vote was the goal. Neither of them are quality with the choice of being the lesser of two evils before the voters. The question asked can't be answered with a short answer. It's very complicated. Part two to follow." "Why do politicians want to divide? Simple Answer. Political Power. How do we overcome? For the actions of elected officials, pretty simple. Term Limits at the same level of peaceful enthusiasm as those misfits on Jan. 6. For the rest of the human race. Answer. The second coming of the lord."*

**The Lone Conservative in Hall County, Georgia:** *"David. Your observation is on point! Pop culture is a major contributor of racism and why it is a contentious subject? Pop culture even adds to sexism. People are conditioned. I have witnessed plenty of folks getting conditioned in my early days in media as an actor, editor, filmmaker. It's why I turned to media as a conservative. I lived in Saudi Arabia as a government contractor from 2002 to 2004 and then a short stent in 2006. There my trainees from the Royal Saudi Air Force explained their view about the United States. It was all media narratives including racism that existed in America. So, I thought why can't I* *voice my values in story because Hollywood doesn't have it right from the Americans I am with. I digress... "Institutional Racism" is a very strange slippery slope in hopes of addressing it. It is mentioned at the height of the civil rights era. I work for what I earn. I don't believe it was handed to me because of my skin. Lord's will first and foremost. Earned by kindness, sweat, blood, tears, mentor, love etc not because of my skin. I was raised in the south and that is how I experienced the world. Institutional Racism is the boogey man (not John Wick). It's an effective mind trick that gets everyone in a tizzy and preys upon insecurities. It certainly divides. As far as picking a candidate...I think as a party, we show always pick the candidate that best represents the ideology of conservatism. (BTW Prager does a great job explaining conservatism if ever in a conversation with a liberal LOL). From what I understand, Walker won the primary.... Voting is a totally separate contentious subject  😊 !"*

**David:** *The Lone Conservative in Hall County, Georgia Understand, but can it be minimized? Yes, it can one step at a time. There are many other reasons besides what is being talked about here. First step would a term limits amendment. That would be a monumental task to say the least, but a worthy goal American politics is rooted in a moderate voice where compromise is necessary for effective government. The moderate voice has disappeared from American Politics. Haven't seen or observed any political leadership from either party that pushes for a moderate voice. I hear words, but no actions, hence the need for term limits.*

**The Lone Conservative in Hall County, Georgia:** *"So much racism depends on where you are. I have worked and lived in very diverse places around the United States and the world. There are places where I have been that for some reason people engage in not recognizing the humanity varying several degrees in cruelty because of their skin tone. I have been in places where the skin tone varied from albino to dark black and we regard ourselves as family. Racism will mostly like rear its ugly head no matter what. But it not as common anymore. My family history attest to that. I haven't gotten to know any politicians that utilize racism as tool (but I have only been directly involved in the GOP for near 2 years. Voted out of my chair... LOL! And now running rouge LOL!) I would probably not engage in a politician like that if I had sensed it. They are representative of all the people. Perhaps that is the concept that all people need to keep in mind to overcome racism. Politicians represent us! We the people. White, Black, Latino, Asian, Georgia Tech Fan, etc. Ignore the overt practices of the mainstream media (the harpies). There is a children's bible song that always comes to* *mind "Be careful little eyes what you see". I believe we just get caught up in hype of racism. It's certainly not something you are born with."*

***John:*** *"#1 racial divide is politics, "#2 racial divide cultural and "#3 is how you were raised and developed as an individual. Your choice as you get older to decide on how you see people. It's hard when white people choose to hate and black people choose hate not to take a side, but there is a difference when people look at other races and decide on your opinion of how they act. Not the entire race, but how they act toward each other as minorities (any race) and how you react!"*

***The Lone Conservative in Hall County, Georgia:*** *"John, to add I think there is huge economic divide that adds to the turmoil. Two broke men comparing themselves and trying to make ends meet; fight each other and never having the realization that they are both destitute because of this. That greed makes the world go around."*

David, John, and the Lone Conservative had a few comments that stood out to us. The first by David is that people don't take responsibility for their actions anymore. That is sad that so many people want to blame others for their own mistakes. The problem is there is no respect in our country anymore. People are just evil and want others to take the blame for racism in America. The Lone Conservative talks about term limits and how that might help bring this topic out in the open and start the healing process that this nation needs. We talked about term limits in a previous chapter. We agree there must be term limits put in place for all elected politicians, no matter what office they are elected to. John made a point about culture. This country has an unlimited cultural background and a storied past with immigrants coming through Ellis Island to start the process of becoming United States citizens. As Americans, we must respect other cultures and understand the way we are brought up and stop the hate just because someone doesn't understand our individual culture. We just want to add that as parents we must stop raising our children to hate the colors of their neighbors' skin. Every race must stop doing this and maybe, just maybe in a few short years, we can eliminate racism altogether. Wouldn't that be amazing!!

***Joseph:*** *"To many cultures in America, they are colliding because Obama-hole started this race war. Black voters thought he will help them rise and he did nothing. He is a Muslim. Degraded the blacks over 8 years. Now we have a dementia fool who doesn't know where he is all the time. He spread promises to get people to vote. Free* *this free that. Once he stole the election, he fucked you. Hasn't done nothing so far, created more racism and bias among the cultures. The democraps fault. Power, greed, corruption all over. America is cowing to a great civil war, a revolution. You can't trust the democrap government. High gas, high crime, high food, high inflation, high bias, high racism, stolen elections, highest corruption ever."*

**Rabun County GA Republican Party:** *"I'd love to have an adult discussion about this."*

We believe we all would and hopefully these comments can help us move forward as a united nation, instead of a divided country ready for another Civil War.

**Bill:** *"Well, first of all, I do not believe it is just the politicians. I am sorry to say that I believe there is still a large segment of "The people" who have issues with racism."*

Bill is right, but that is where it starts.

**David:** *"There are many reasons there is so much racism in America today. I would start with one of the most important historical reasons, namely, the need to morally justify Indian-killing and slavery. How can otherwise moral people bring themselves to engage in moral atrocities like enslaving Africans and massacring Indians? No one wants to think of themselves as monsters, so when they do monstrous things, they need some kind of excuse or justification to make it seem okay. From the very beginnings of our history, racism has provided that justification. The racist belief that black people and Native Americans are racially inferior was essential to slavery and westward expansion. Since America's slavery and westward expansion went on for more than 200 years, racist ideas had generation after generation after generation in which to become rooted in the American psyche."*

**Sean:** *"There's no racism in America, only racism that there is political, and people fall for it There're just a****** people and good people."*

**Tom:** *"It might be cynical to simply say "politicians play their divide and conquer games", but we have to accept it is there mixed in with other motives. I do think identity politics is always problematic, and majority white identity politics is worse because it preys on people's fears, but I don't know if they see it purely as racial, and "white identity" politics isn't just for whites, but preys on a reverse victim* *status. What is cynical there is the idea that anything that the government does to help ALL PEOPLE also helps the wrong sort of people, undeserving people. And the "solution" is always to pretend colorblind, pretend away inequality of opportunity, pretend away real racism, pretend that the only way forward is to ignore all categories except money. So, money is the only status that matters, and if you have it, you earned it, and others want to take it away, so you have to stop them. So even if you don't HAVE money now, someday you will, and you don't want to let part of it (via taxes) helps undeserving people".*

**Paul:** *"We will never end racism, I'm 62 and not much has changed since i was 10, in some areas of the country it's still huge, like the old lady screaming at BLM members I'm gonna teach my grandchildren to hate each and every one of you, with such venom in her voice, you knew she taught her kids to hate. I saw my black friends get treated differently at 10 and I've seen them get treated the same at 62. Someone knocked the rocks over and allowed these ^#$%/$^ to have a voice, now you see that someone dining with a white supremacist and an antisemite, and people are perfectly ok with it, that's a problem."*

**Dennis:** *"Why? because the political left can, and have, used the boogeyman of 'racism' in a divide and conquer strategy...they created the myth of the raging white supremacist, of the MAGA extremist who are 'gonna put ya'll back in chains' according to Joe Biden... Racism is a tool the political left uses to carry on with their campaign of fear and divisiveness in the black, brown, and Asian communities..."*

**Elizabeth:** *Racism is a thing now because it is used as a tool to divide us. It's intentional. And I am sick of it. All my life, I never looked at an individual and immediately had a reaction because of his race.... We are all part of the human race, God's perfect creation. I am angry and saddened by the intentional divide caused in America. We are being destroyed from within by those who hold the power.*

**Liz:** *"We didn't have racism until Obama started the great divide. He set us back 50 yrs. when it comes to race relations."*

**Paul:** *"Our laws are not racist, and our country is no different than the rest of the world (excluding Muslim countries, Russia, China, North Korea) There are a few more but America is not on the list."*

**Michael:** *"The only racism I see is from a certain ethnic group that has been misled into believing every white person is a racist and hates their guts. The liberal/dems have convinced them that the conservatives hate their guts when they just want to go on with their lives and be left alone. Just my opinion and what I have observed."*

**_Madeleine:_** _"Because racism is just ignorance, and you can never irradicate ignorance it will always be a work in progress."_

**_Scotty:_** _"Like a negative outlook has of innocence, until there is a political reason for politician to care about them. The 98% conviction rate in LA, or the thousands of bodies piled up because of crime in Chicago, it doesn't matter because the people in those community's aren't involved in policy making. They've been embezzling money since the foundation of government, and without education it can never be fixed. If the individual doesn't 'clean up their act' so to speak, there won't ever be wide scale change. Change yourself and you create an upward spiral of positive change, because we are all interwoven connected, even in the smallest ways. Get Educated, develop skills, help your family, save the world on life, racism can be seen everywhere. It's a question of how many ways can you divide and group, or any number of groups. They can be infinitely divided by any number of things."_

**_Ida:_** _"This is the way to end our "United" States and start the one world dominance that the wealthy ten percent are working towards. We can't play into their game and allow that to happen. The ones that are uneducated and raised to be suspicious of anyone who's, not like them are playing right into their hands. And if they really followed the teachings of their God, this wouldn't even be an issue because we're taught to love everyone as we love ourselves. Also, to take care of one another."_

Racism doesn't only occur in the United States. It's all over the world today. The only way we will ever slow it down and hopefully stop it is being **_UNITED_**. We have said that word (United) several times throughout this book and we really believe it's the only way to move into the future. Politicians are ruining our country from the inside and we the people are the only ones to stop that. We only have two chapters left and we will be done. In our next Chapter we want to talk about some great men and women of the United States of America, which is our amazing Veterans. We will leave you with this last quote.

**_Kawika:_** _"Racism is so intertwined in society today that whole nations would fail if we are able to remove it from society. It has influenced Church and State and has been the driving force behind western capitalism declaring who is and who is not worthy. The unraveling of centuries of lies will cause as much bloodshed as the original lie!!! That being supremacy!!!"_

# Chapter 11

# "Our Veterans"

Tell me why you think all veterans of foreign wars should receive a government retirement every month until their death.

Tell me why you think they should be exempt from paying state and federal taxes, or why they shouldn't.

This is your time to recognize your veteran. Tell us about him or her and branch of service and if they were deployed to a foreign war. And add a story they may have told you!

We are getting so close to finishing this book. We told you these chapters would be easy to read. In this chapter we wanted people to talk about our veterans. Give them a chance to answer a few questions and tell us about *their* veteran. We believe that all veterans are heroes. Veterans, me included, leave our families behind and protect the citizens of the United States of America. We don't do it for the glory or because we want to fight wars, we serve because we are patriotic and love this country. Unfortunately, sometimes a country must go to war to protect its assets. When we went to Afghanistan, that was their people destroying the World Trade Center in New York City and our Pentagon. We lost a total of just under three thousand people that day. We were sent to Iraq in 1991 because we were protecting another country and an ally where Saddam Hussain the president of Iraq wanted to invade, which was Kuwait. Our military personnel were sent to Iraq in 2003 because intelligence agencies said Hussain had weapons of mass destruction. None of us went to war because we wanted to. Our politicians, the ones who cower behind their desks and make decisions for the rest of us, sent your loved ones into harm's way. The War on Terrorism is past its twentieth year, with no end in sight. The problem is that we will always have bad apples who want to destroy our way of life, from foreign terrorists to domestic terrorists. People just don't like the United States. We are sure most of us just want to be left alone and be happy, but politicians want chaos in this country because it keeps them in power. They use our veterans to get what they want, every politician is the same. When we do get into conflicts or war, depending on what party holds the executive branch, the other party (republican or democrat) always tells us that we should not be doing this, we should not be involved. However, when their party is in control elected officials of that party vote along with the executive, using our veterans as pawns in their chess game.

Twenty-year wars are not supposed to occur for that long under the Constitution. If we look at Article, I Section 8 under Powers of Congress it says, "To declare War, grant letters of Marque and Reprisal, and make rules concerning Captures on Land and Water." Right after that job responsibility, the very next line it states this: "to raise and support Armies, but no Appropriation of Money to that use shall be for a longer Term of two Years." Hell, these Congressional cowards won't even declare war anymore. They are weak-minded people, and most do nothing to support veterans. But they will support impeachment hearings, and give money to the National Institute of Health, headed by Dr. Fauci until his retirement. They spent millions of dollars on their January sixth hearing, but they hardly do much to take care of our veterans. The funny part is that no one sees it; we have had republican and democrat congressional members vote no on veterans' bills. Try passing a veteran's bill with help just for veterans without adding on additional money for other programs. They never do stand-alone legislation; they always want to add additional spending that doesn't pertain to veterans. We are living in a misguided, misdirected country, and that is sad.

This country must take care of our veterans for the following reasons. First, they volunteered to serve and follow orders to ensure the United States has peace and tranquility. We do not want wars here in America, so we need to keep the people who want to harm us somewhere else. We do not have a draft system anymore and, according to experts, our military faces the largest hurdle in recruiting in half a century. In an article published in Bloomberg Government by Roxana Tron, "The U.S. depends on strong, all-volunteer forces to carry out its foreign policy and defend strategic interests. Military leaders often say their services are only as good as their people. With operations shifting to the realms of cyber, artificial intelligence, and hypersonic weapons, and China and Russia challenging U.S. leadership globally, the lack of qualified recruits could become a fundamental national security handicap." She went on to say, "The Army is facing the most acute recruiting problems. The service will finish fiscal 2022 with about 466,000 active-duty soldiers—10,000 people below target, according to Lt. Gen. Douglas Stitt, the Army's deputy chief of staff for personnel." Should another major conflict happen, and, on a few fronts, they will reinstitute the draft. Those are a few reasons why we must ensure our veterans' needs come first before illegal immigrants.

Most politicians, if not all, live in affluent areas of their community, living a great lifestyle that most people can't afford. When they go into restaurants, we believe sometimes their meals are comped, meaning they don't pay for their food. Restaurant owners hope to one day get favors from these politicians who frequent their establishments. You would not believe all the benefits these politicians get. If we had time, we would get into them. You are most likely wondering where we are going with this, and we want to show you what our politicians get for doing basically nothing for this country. That leads us to what we want to talk about in this chapter and that is ***VETERAN HOMELESSNESS.*** This is a serious issue for veterans that politicians will not confront. They make sure they get their money but nothing for our veterans who are homeless. There are states and activists for the homeless, who do actually help with this issue, but we feel not enough is being done by tyrants in Washington or even politicians in each sovereign state. Data shows that over thirty-three thousand veterans are homeless, when one is too many. We find it's sad that politicians have funded our money for a wall around President Biden's beach front home in Delaware, which is the right thing to do, we must keep our presidents safe. But politicians will spend our tax money on everything except a safe place where veterans don't have to stay out in the elements. You can't tell us that this government can't build a small community for homeless veterans in every state. We believe they can. They waste money on so many projects, it's time to start taking care of we the people, especially discharged veterans.

Here in South Carolina, we have approximately 460 veterans who are homeless. Let us show you a few more states with high veterans' homelessness. Florida has over 2,400, Colorado over 1,000, and Oregon 1,400-plus. In our previous state of residence, New York, they have over 1,200 homeless veterans, and in the very liberal state of California, there are more than 10,000 veterans living on the streets. Every state in this union has homeless veterans that deserve a place to live. These statistics were from 2020, so numbers may not match today, some states will be lower and some higher. These states can also build a community for Veterans. When I (Dennis) served in Iraq, we lived in small housing units designed for two soldiers. It was not the best housing situation; it should have been one soldier to a room. They were about six feet wide by twenty feet long. They were metal housing units and had the luxuries of home, with lights, air conditioning, and heat; the basic needs we all want. There must be a way for our federal government to send money to each state to build these small communities that will keep our veterans safe. Maybe we can end veterans' homelessness together. One veteran at a time.

We always think about veterans and daily both authors of this book thank several for their service, from World War II to present day wars. They deserve our recognition for the freedoms we have. As we were writing this very chapter, we got lucky and received an unexpected gift. This was on our United States Constitutional Group on Facebook, and it could not have come at a better time. This poem is not only for Christmas but for every day of the year. This represents what not only soldiers must endure but every branch of our military. The individual who wrote this poem had only one request. To send it to as many people as possible. We say, let's make him famous. Grab a tissue, it will fill your eyes up, just like it did ours. This is another reason why we need to ensure homeless veterans have a place to feel safe. Enjoy this great poem!!

T'was the night before Christmas,
he lived all alone,
in a one-bedroom house,
made of plaster and stone.

I had come down the chimney,
with presents to give,
and to see just who,
in this home, did live.

I looked all about,
a strange sight I did see,
no tinsel, no presents,
not even a tree.

No stocking by mantle,
just boots filled with sand,
on the wall hung pictures,
of far distant lands.

With medals and badges,
awards of all kinds,
a sober thought,
came through my mind.

For this house was different,
it was dark and dreary,
I found the home of a soldier,
once I could see clearly.

The soldier lay sleeping,
silent, alone,
curled up on the floor,
in this one bedroom home.

The face was so gentle,
the room in disorder,
not how I pictured,
a true modern soldier.

Was this the hero,
of whom I'd just read?
Curled up on a poncho,
the floor for a bed?

I realized the families,
that I saw this night,
owed their lives to these soldiers,
who were willing to fight.

Soon round the world,
the children would play,
and grownups would celebrate,
a bright Christmas day.

They all enjoyed freedom,
each month of the year,
because of the soldiers,
like the one lying here.

I couldn't help wonder,
how many lay alone,
on a cold Christmas eve,
in a land far from home.

The very thought brought,
a tear to my eye,
I dropped to my knees,
and started to cry.

The soldier awakened,
and I heard a rough voice,
"Santa, don't cry,
this life is my choice;

I fight for freedom,
I don't ask for more,
my life is my god,
my country, my corps."

The soldier rolled over,
and drifted to sleep,
I couldn't control it,
I continued to weep.

I kept watch for hours,
so silent and still,
and we both shivered,
from the cold night's chill.

I did not want to leave,
on that cold, dark, night,
this guardian of honor,
so willing to fight.

Then the soldier rolled over,
with a voice soft and pure,
whispered, "Carry on, Santa,
it's Christmas day, all is secure."

One look at my watch,
and I knew he was right.
"Merry Christmas, my friend,
and to all a good night."

This poem was written by a Peacekeeping soldier stationed overseas. The following is his request. I think it is reasonable.

*PLEASE. Would you do me the kind favor of sending this to as many people as you can? Christmas will be coming soon, and some credit is due to all the service men and women for our being able to celebrate these festivities. Let's try in this small way to pay a tiny bit of what we owe. Make people stop and think of our heroes, living and dead, who sacrificed themselves for us. Please, do your small part to plant this small seed.*

I (Dennis Gravelle) served in the New York Army National Guard as a photojournalist with the 138th Public Affairs Detachment. We were a small group of soldiers who deployed to FOB Courage in Mosul, Iraq, late in 2005. We were weekend warriors, not trained soldiers like the full-time Army guys.

We shot photos most of the time, but we came together and created a small piece of history that will stay with us until the time we leave this Earth. We had our small cliques, print media on one side and broadcast journalism on the other. Some of us didn't like others, but we came together to complete a mission. I have good stories and I have some bad stories, and kept a journal, writing in it every day until our unit was deployed back to the States. Maybe that will be my next book, not sure yet. I am sure there is a lot of material that should not get out because of those good and bad days, and I said whatever was on my mind. We also had a few higher-ranking soldiers who could not perform to command standards. Great guys, and enjoy their company, but our leaders didn't feel they could lead soldiers. That left two lower-ranking soldiers running each unit. As an E-5 Sergeant, I was helping the print section and we had an E-6 Staff Sergeant running the broadcast section. We didn't have the best of experience either, but we made it work. It worked because of the soldiers we had, making it a success. Our print section wrote several stories about soldiers and their missions in and around Mosul.

We were attached for most of our deployment with the 172$^{nd}$ Stryker Brigade from Alaska and these soldiers welcomed us, well, most of us, with open arms. For me, writing stories about these soldiers made my job easier and extremely rewarding. I remember my first mission with a team led by Staff Sgt. Paul Volino. I was already nervous because this was my first time going outside the wire, and I remembered a few days earlier when landing in Mosul, within twelve hours, even before reaching FOB Courage, our convoy was hit with an Improvised Explosive Device (IED). Luckily, I was in the last vehicle, and no one died. The Stryker vehicle I was in had a soldier in a turret. He lowered his head and calmly told us what was happening and said, "Just follow my lead." If he hadn't been so calm, I think things would have had a very different outcome. When we got to FOB Courage, we saw what the IED did to one vehicle, and I think that woke us up to the reality of what could happen. As soldiers, you still must complete the mission, so no matter the outcome we had to go outside the wire and get the job done. Volino introduced himself to my partner and me and got me feeling comfortable, asking my partner and me if we wanted to pull air guard to give his guys a break. I had no idea what it was, at first, but after he explained it, I said Hell, yes! and my partner declined. So, there I was pulling air guard for a unit that didn't know me, and that day I earned some respect. Volino and his soldiers were an amazing group, and I had the pleasure of giving a soldier a break and pulling air guard. If I had to do it again, I would not even hesitate. That is how much respect I have for those soldiers.

One other soldier I want to mention is Sgt. Tom Wheeler. He ended up being my partner and my roommate. Another stand-up person who made the Army his career. I haven't talked with him in a while, but just like cousins, we could pick up where we left off. We made a great team; he was the broadcast guy and me the print guy, we complimented each other. Most print and broadcast guys don't get along but having him as a friend and roommate proved two soldiers who didn't know each other could be very successful, and we were. I specifically remember one night patrol we went on with Sgt. Volino and his crew. Wheeler and I were informed by Volino that we would be his rear security guards, of course I had to inform him that I had never done that—I shot photos. He said, "You are a soldier first, and I trust that you both can do the job." We did rear security that night and we each had a great time. Not only do I want to thank Volini and Wheeler, but I also want to thank all the other soldiers of the 138th Public Affairs Detachment. We all came together, and it was an honor serving with all of you.

Every soldier of the 138th came back in one piece, well there were a few issues that I am sure we will never talk about, but for some, coming to terms with soldiers killed in action was the hardest time for not only the unit's but for each of us. When a soldier dies, a soldier memorial is performed, where their buddies talk about how they felt about him or her and their commanding officers also gets the opportunity to say something about his soldier. They were more like family to each other, and I could tell the loss hurt. It was a very emotional time for everyone there. My job was to take photos and write an article about the comments that were said. It was never easy doing that, but again, we got through it. Let's see how others feel about those questions that I asked.

***Manny:*** *"They should get something in Return for their service., if we give it to immigrants and illegals, which we shouldn't., unless of a disability., but should give a percentage down to four or five years., 75%-30yrs 50%-20yrs 25%-10yrs 10%-5yrs …, just a thought"*

**_Jerald:_** _"As a veteran of 20 years in Army I don't believe in most of what you said I didn't join to get rich. I used education benefits both before and after I retired. Maybe tax-free income up to minimum wages. Many Generals walk into high paying situations upon retirement. Enlisted not so much. Medical after retirement should be covered which it was when I initially retired. Then came Bill and Hillary came along and changed it where we had to pay. Luckily, I had started a successful business. I don't want to be seen as greedy the VA does a pretty good job of taking care of disabled veterans one thing, I don't think is right when we turn 65 Medicare is first payer. Just my thoughts."_

**_Julius:_** _"When I become president all veterans that have served in combat will never be homeless! I will designate a place for the veterans with a nice home(house) and benefits they can receive on free of charge. They will have their own community directed with their own laws and officials. They'll have the opportunity to grow out of the community if they choose and be prosperous. Grandfather and uncle was a veteran, they did not comment their service._

**_Tami:_** _As a veteran myself I am going to answer these. I served in the US Navy from 2003 to 2008. While I never step foot in the hot zone, I supported from the zones that dropped the bombs earned my combat pin._

_1. I signed up to serve of my own free will as a job. It is not the governments place to pay my paycheck the rest of my life, listen up Congress members this should apply to you as well._

_2. I think if you are over a certain percentage disabled from your service. 10% is okay with me I say start paying less taxes_

**_Nicki:_** _"1. As a veteran, I don't believe Veterans should receive a retirement benefit unless they choose to serve long enough to retire. Veterans like myself, my mom, and my older brother who left the Service before retirement do not deserve to be paid for the rest of our lives. My father, however, chose to serve 31 years and earned his retirement benefits from the military. My younger brother has chosen to serve until he retires as well. Financially speaking, it's a smart move._

_2. I'm open to the idea of tax breaks for veterans but I'd like to hear exactly how it would work. Do you have to serve a particular number of years to qualify? Does it matter what kind of discharge you have?_

_3. Both of my parents deployed with the Army during Desert Shield and Desert Storm. Due to their specific MOS's, they were among the first to deploy and among the last to return. As a kid, it was incredibly hard to have both of my parents deployed_ *to a war zone at the same time. My mom was an Arabic linguist and she told me stories of her time working with families fleeing the violence as well as soldiers who would willingly turn themselves over to American forces seeking shelter, food, and medical attention. My dad was in EOD and told us stories about how they would go out in front of other troops to search or IEDs and other explosives. He told a particular story about finding abandoned bunkers from enemy soldiers where they would leave everything from their weapons to blankets, like they just gave up and walked back to their homes"*

***Richard:*** *1. There is retirement for veterans, is called doing 20 years. There's also disability that's given to veterans if medical eligibility is met. I also happen to believe there should be safety nets for all citizens and don't think offering basic necessities for survival should be a recruitment tool, but here we are*

*2. I'm fine with exemption from certain taxes for some arbitrary number that'd decided.*

*3. I was in the marines from 2005 to 2012 and deployed to Iraq in 2008 and trained with marines of other countries in 2011*

***Kyle:*** *I think the above veterans are absolutely right on question one. We all served voluntarily. If a state wants to exempt veterans from paying state taxes, that's fine, but Federal taxes, no. U.S. Navy 1995 - 2001.*

***Peggy:*** *"Answer to #1 - People in the Armed forces who served in wars and/or 5 years or more should receive a lifetime pension because they literally put their life on the line to serve.*

*Answer to # 2 - I think they should receive reduced taxes for serving.*

*Answer #3 - My grandfather served in WWI - my dad and uncles in WWII - one uncle during Korean war - one cousin in Vietnam - cousins in Afghanistan & Iraq. Thankfully they all returned - but all who serve in war - walk through hell."*

***Mark:*** *"Personally, I support our veterans and the many others who have participated in public service. I do have a special place in my heart for all people who served in our military, whether they served in combat or not. Many of us were never assigned to combat zones, but know those who were, including people who were prisoners of war. I am not sure how best to help veterans with taxes, but veterans should receive a retirement benefit until their death. The federal government and states waste enough money that veterans who served in combat should be tax exempt from state and federal taxes. In the long run, I believe this would actually save taxpayers money, because there would not be as many homeless veterans and/or veterans that suffer from various types* *of mental illness. Dennis, I think you know why many do not like to discuss their personal experiences. I will add however, that many members of my family have served, starting with my father, and three of his four brothers. God Bless – "*

**Patty** replied to **Mark** saying: *"I agree. Veterans should get the same benefits the useless career politicians get."*

*Rachael: "Yes! No veteran should be homeless period."*

*Jerry: "I'm a veteran, Dennis. I served and felt honored to serve. With respect to your multipart question, here's the deal. I paid taxes while I was in. My wife and I could have qualified for food stamps given my rate of pay. But we paid taxes. And should have. Vets of wars come back in varied different states and to varied different lives. If you served, you took the same oath that I took. It had to do with giving myself to the Constitution and to more senior officers and to the nation. There was nothing in the agreement with respect to keeping us solvent until death. It just didn't. But I did it.*

*I understand that you are empathetic towards vets who fought in wars that our politicians decided to send others to. I do. But there's this thing, and it's this: when you sign up, you sign up. You sign up for whatever comes to you.*

*I never had a sense that the government, or anyone else, should pay me until I die. That's not the way it works. The way it SHOULD work is that people who care donate their time, effort, and funds to groups that take care of our veterans."*

*Karen: "Yes, they deserve monthly retirement checks. Anything if will prevent veteran homelessness. Multiple reasons why Vets may have difficulty with civilian life. I believe tax exemption for the military monthly retirement money and half taxes for income tax regardless of income bracket or perhaps greater degrees of tax exemption for those who stayed in longer. So, 50% tax cut plus 1% additional for each year served. So, if you served 20 years, then you get 70% income tax exemption/reduction. This encourages longer serving and strengthen our military as many will go for 4 years and retire after this for civilian life."*

*William: "Our Great Vet's. Shouldn't Have to pay For Jack S... They've Paid Enough. Our Country Don't Care about Them, The Youth and the Needy whether Elderly or 14 and Disabled. We Give it All away to Those who never Worked a Damn Day to help Our Country. It's Surely Time We Fight Back with Everything We've Got Good People! I For One, am Beyond Sick of This Loss! God Bless American's. Who Deserve It. GEN. TYLER."*

***Steven:*** *"1) Under the current structure, I'm on board with the disability payments (if that's what you're calling "retirement"). There could be some more clearly defined ways to tabulate these payments so they can actually be budgeted for, but this is also smart business because most of these recruits are trained to topple governments so it's best to keep them as reluctant allies than cast them aside and make enemies of them. Another option could be to give them all much larger salaries and make them sign waivers (just throwing out a libertarian answer since you posted in a libertarian group).*

*2) Of course, their income should be tax exempt! And so should everyone else's. Taxation should be voluntary, so taxing only at the point of sale is the only way to achieve this.*

*3) I'm not going to name names, but I've heard stories of trading life savers (the MRE version) for weeks to afford a soccer ball and goals for some local kids, skipping nap time after days long missions so they can bring some bottled water and candy to local kids, and I've also heard tales of handing over duffle bags of money to build $10k wells that were never built and throwing $100s of thousands of equipment overboard at sea so they can have a larger budget approved for next year. This era of military service is certainly not for the faint of heart and the level of care the VA is known for is downright criminal."*

**Peter's** reply to **Steven:** *"An additional option: Amend the United States Constitution prohibiting the Administration and Congress from deploying Our Armed Forces to any foreign country. Moreover, eliminate the concept of "Protected Territories." If a people refuse to become a state, then, don't waste resources on them. Vis-a-vis Puerto Rico, Guam, etc."*

***Darlene:*** *"An additional option: Amend the United States Constitution prohibiting the Administration and Congress from deploying Our Armed Forces to any foreign country. Moreover, eliminate the concept of "Protected Territories." If a people refuse to become a state, then, don't waste resources on them. Vis-a-vis Puerto Rico, Guam, etc."*

***Bert:*** *"Veterans should receive what they were promised when they signed up. They should receive treatments and services for the effects they experienced due to mental and or physical trauma. There was never a promise to be tax free. Veterans already get special consideration for government jobs, housing, and discounts within our society. The concept of serving is service to the nation. Not to receive special treatment from the nation for life."*

***Lola:*** *"I've known vets from WWII to present day. They all come back changed. They come back to various civilian circumstances. Some have a place, and some don't. Some have physical and mental challenges. One size fits all payments may not fit all. Housing allowance, food stamps, for those who need it all tax free. Lifetime full coverage healthcare not just for use at the VA. Retraining for civilian employment. Reduced taxes based on years of service for earned income. When they retire, a boost in SSI payments."*

*"I was born in 1954. Before the war one guy operated a cat but the sound of them after the war made him edgy. Another man was affected when planes flew over. My brother-in-law was in Viet Nam and effected by agent orange. He died of complications. A co-worker spent years looking for his brother and was notified years later of his death due to exposer less than 100 miles away. Homeless, suicides, even the way the VA deals with vets, we can do better."*

I wish we had those veterans names so we could honor them, like we do all other Military personnel across this world.

We didn't get anyone who wanted to tell us their stories but that's alright. Like one comment said, veterans don't do this for recognition or fame, they serve because they love this country and will ensure every citizen of America can be free and dream of better things to come. We want to thank everyone for these comments, and we thank all of you who have served not only in a foreign war, but all military deployed in this country and around the world, including their families. We will end this chapter on this last quote, which makes a lot of sense.

***Linda:*** *"We need to take better care of our veterans than BLM & immigrants!! case closed!!!"*

# Chapter 12

# "Stand United"

Have you ever considered switching to a different political party?

What type of party would you be interested in joining if you did switch?

We hear people every day saying they can't stand the republican and democratic parties any longer. They are too corrupt and out of touch with American citizens. They say they want a change but don't know where to turn. In this chapter, Jack and I will tell you ways we are trying to bring Patriots together to ***"Stand United."*** It is our belief that both major parties have taken our country as far as they can. Due to their partisan ***"GRIDLOCK"*** they have driven this beautiful country to a roadblock, and neither party knows how to put our country back on the path again. With party politics our representatives are not independent thinkers and will only ensure their party gets the win. The only people who lose in the long run are we the people.

Before we go further into this topic let's review the Declaration of Independence: "We hold these truths to be self-evident, that all men are created equal, that they are endowed by their Creator with certain unalienable Rights, that among these are Life, Liberty and the pursuit of Happiness.—That to secure these rights, Governments are instituted among Men, deriving their just powers from the consent of the governed." Read that last sentence again and that tells us the men and women we elect get their powers from we, the people. "That whenever any Form of Government becomes destructive of these ends, it is the Right of the People to alter or to abolish it, and to institute new Government." That is telling us that we have the power and right to change this government to the way we see fit.

This government of today has become tyrannical and needs to be altered. We all know that and yet we continue to let this government have control over us. We know that people fear the government and have lost sight of the fact that the government belongs to us. Unfortunately, we have re-elected the same people to office for years and years. Now that they have the power, they will do anything they can to keep their thumbs on all of us to keep us in line. Seventy-five percent of people feel we are heading in the wrong direction and seven out of ten registered voters want a new party that represents a new era of politicians who are independent and governed by the constitution. People are sick and tired of the democratic and republican parties, yet we still vote for these parties because we are told lies and misinformation about America and most people buy into the hype. It's time to stop believing the hypocrites and form a coalition that will pave a path for all Citizens, not just the privileged.

What has the republican party done to help middle- and lower-class working Americans get decent paying wages? They talk about it every year; nothing has been achieved. Elect us and things will get better, they say.

What has the democratic party done to raise wages for their constituents and struggling families? They could have passed legislation over the past two years. Our wages have barely moved the last few years and we state with confidence that raises have not kept up with inflation. The democratic party held all branches of government from 2020-2022. They tell us they want fifteen dollars an hour for minimum wage, so why has nothing been passed? They could have done it but there was no movement on legislation increasing wages. They also tell constituents, elect us and things will get better. Guess what people—it hasn't got any better. They tell constituents to elect them, and things will get better and when we do they say we don't have enough votes to make it a reality, so we will try again in two years, so you must vote for us then. Reality never happens, people. It's time to wake up and smell the coffee. In our opinion, people haven't done better since Reagan was our president. Every elected president since then has not delivered for the American people.

That is both republican and democratic presidential administrations. They have failed this country in more ways than we can count.

We need to ask this question: why do we keep believing these political tyrants when we all know they fail us daily? We already know that both parties have run this country into the ground, but we keep giving them another chance. How many more chances are we going to give them, when we have given them too many already. Are we the people that dumb and stupid? That's what politicians think we are. When we keep electing the same people into office every two to four years on a silver platter, they think they can do whatever they want to you. After all, you keep reelecting them so we must be dumb and stupid or maybe we are just blindsided, brainwashed by them when they say, "This is the way." What is it going to take for the people of this country to pull our heads out of our assess and say, "No more"? Or don't you care that you are being taken advantage of, with both parties slowly taking our rights and freedoms away?

How much longer are we the people going to put up with these incompetent congressional members with all the failures of this country? An elected politician's responsibility is to unify this country so every American, no matter what race, religion or beliefs are, so we can enjoy the rights and freedoms guaranteed under the United States Constitution. Our tyrants only create division, for they fear a unified people. What can we do as average working people to get united?

We the people of America know one thing and that is we are falling behind every day, thanks to this two-party system of control. Black Americans, Asian Americans, White Americans, male and female alike, we are all frustrated and annoyed with the political tyrants. We need to stand up and become a force to be reckoned with. We cannot bow our heads down in disgrace any longer. The more time we put off reclaiming our country, the less time we have to rebuild it, and make it a country where everyone prospers. Not just certain people in society, but everyone in society. Every one of us must become hawks in this country, that is full of political asses and elephants. The devil himself is here and trying to tear down this United States.

We have lost faith in our Almighty God, and we must stop the devil from winning. We need to be a country of Patriots that helps restore faith in America. One thing we don't have is time; we must unite everyone as quickly as we can over the next two years under a new banner, with a new name in politics. We must form a coalition of Patriots who want to run for office. That time has come, that time is now. There are many political parties out there that are trying to gain traction, yet not one has really made the grade. Most are just spin-offs of the republican and democratic parties who must abide by their rules. How does that make a difference in politics? Just a bunch of pissed-off people who became sick and tired of them both. The old way of conducting politics is over, the old guard must step aside and hand the reins over to a new alliance, a new party that looks at politics differently. A party that is by the people, for the people. No matter what color we are, where we live, or how much we make. We do it because it's time we all come together and unite against tyranny. Our constitution isn't perfect—that, we all know—however, it is better than any other constitution out there in the world. The problem now, here today, is that politicians have lost sight of that fact, that is why Patriots must reel the line back in and recast it out to find new candidates for office that stand united with "we the people," not with political parties. We are calling on all Patriots to help us form that coalition to retake America from these tyrants we have and let a new breed of talented people (Patriots) to move this country forward. People who believe in God and restoring faith in our communities. People who love our country because of the opportunity it presents, and a plan is created where no one is left behind.

We are not saying that everyone is fed up with politics, and some people like to be brainwashed and that is fine if you want to be a follower and not a leader. You may like being that person who sits on the couch watching that idiot box (television) and enjoys listening to one-sided news media outlets, who never give you the full story or quote. They pick and choose what they want to spoon-feed you to keep you from being totally informed. If that's you, that's fine. However, if you are truly pissed and frustrated with politics you are not alone. There are millions just like us. Jack and I are putting this grassroots coalition together called the Independent Constitutional Party, which we will explain in a minute. We know that we have an uphill battle to overcome, but this is something bigger than us, something we must do for future generations so they can enjoy the same freedoms we had growing up, in a country without dictators and tyrants putting the people down as if we are stupid, ignorant morons. In our opinion, this government decided to try their takeover on the wrong generation, and it's time to say no. Here is the start of our Independent Constitutional Party.

The people of this party will swear allegiance to the direction laid out in the first document of this country, The Declaration of Independence. This document was written for the people to have inalienable rights that include

Life, Liberty, and Pursuit of Happiness, that Men are created equal, and we all have a civic duty to defend these rights. A type of RULE we will consent to so our rights will be protected and preserve. The founding fathers wrote the Declaration of Independence to explain "declaring the causes which impel the American Colonies to the separation."

"This describes the struggle for independence, so we never waiver in the pursuit of independence of the people no matter what generation of America we are at."

Time passing since the revolution has not diminished the onslaught of corrupted people who continue to take away our independence, to the benefit of their own best interest, so our struggle continues.

Secondly, we will swear allegiance to the laws laid out in the next document written by the Framers, The United States Constitution, and the Supreme Law of the Land. The people in congress are supposed to swear and uphold this document when they are elected to office. Today, we face challenges where members obtain positions in three branches of government, who are elected and/or appointed, who do not believe in our type of government. These representatives are willing to govern without referring to the laws of the land and some are trying to abolish the Constitution of the United States. Our Founding Fathers, "mutually pledge to each other our lives, our fortunes, and our sacred honor" and they did, whereas our current administrations have not. The Independent Constitutional Party will stay in contact with the American People to make sure injustices from the government against its constituents are rectified and continue the freedoms from government tyranny as our Founding Fathers had intended. We are not looking to change the existing government; we are attempting to bring America Back to its History. Leaders are to be held accountable to their allegiance of the Oath taken. The laws of the Constitution, already written, not evolving. An evolving Constitution brought down the Roman Empire. If the American people don't stop thinking otherwise, it will bring down America's greatness.

These two documents combined, are the name of this new minor party, The Independent Constitutional Party (ICP), for reasons stated above. Don't fear being an American, embrace our laws and documents that have been put in place for our protection, for our freedom, for our best interest. The Oath taken by the Office for Federal Employees (Senators, Representatives, Political

Appointees and Justices, all military personnel) is as follows and should be embraced throughout his/her appointment:

"I (Name) do solemnly swear (or affirm) that I will support and defend the Constitution of the United States against all enemies foreign and domestic; that I will bear true faith and allegiance to the same; that I take this obligation freely, without any mental reservation or purpose of evasion; and that I will well and faithfully discharge the duties of the office on which I am about to enter, so help me God."

The oath was changed during the Civil War to keep out anyone who was disloyal to the Union. The oath of today has not changed since 1966, and is prescribed in Title 5, section 3331 of the United States Code. The candidate running or representative occupying an office must understand the history of the oath and the importance of its meaning. "Any type of attestation by which an individual signifies that he/she is bound in conscience to perform a particular act truthfully and faithfully; a solemn declaration of truth or obligation." The Oath needs to be upheld, yet most representatives within office today do not know or understand the oath they have taken, which is the cause of our political problems of today.

The President's Oath is written in the United States Constitution. The Oath taken by our President is a s follows:

"I (Name) do solemnly swear (or affirm) that I will faithfully execute the Office of President of the United States, and will to the best of my ability, preserve, protect, and defend the Constitution of the United States."

As the official representative, our current President does not defend, protect, or preserve our Constitution of the United States. But RULES for his own best interest and the interest of the bureaucracies.

Politicians have lost the confidences of *"We the People,"* by using the power granted to them by governing through their own self-interest, a fear James Madison warned us about. The following are eleven injustices of today's politics that this minor party (ICP) would like to justify. Average Americans could provide many more issues, but we will focus on the following ignorance of our leaders today.

Politicians have failed the American citizen by not following their oath of office when elected.

Our government was made to protect the citizens' rights and civil liberties. To govern spending, legislation, and keeping the branches of power separated. It insures rights, prevents the federal government from infringing on these rights, and creates laws. The current representatives have failed the American people by not upholding their Oath. Not understanding its history, its meaning, its purpose. It is their responsibility to give the citizens of this country a fair opportunity to succeed, not to suppress and control them.

Politicians have failed to secure our voting process.

Election fraud has been questioned for many years, our 2020 election being the most questionable. Our Constitutional rights are being infringed upon, the Fifteenth Amendment Section 1; "The right of citizens of the United States to vote shall not be denied or abridged by the United States or by any State on account of race, color, or previous condition of servitude-" Fraudulent elections prevents "We the People," from practicing our American rights to ensure whom is truly voted into office. Previous conditions of servitude, and the lack of personal freedom to make our choices, enabled these politicians to stay in power.

Politicians of today refuse to secure our borders, violating our immigration laws.

It is stated in the Constitution Article 1, Section 8, Clause 4: "(The Congress shall have Power) To establish a uniform Rule of Naturalization, and uniform Laws on the subject of Bankruptcies throughout the United States." Again, infringing on our Constitutional rights.

Politicians have failed to unite our country while creating division among Americans.

Quoted from the Declaration of Independence; "We hold these truths to be self-evident, that all men are created equal, that they are endowed by their Creator with certain inalienable Rights, that among these are Life, Liberty and the pursuit of Happiness.—That to secure these rights, Governments are instituted among Men, deriving their just powers from the consent of the governed,—That whenever any Form of Government becomes destructive of these ends, it is the Right of the People to alter or to abolish it, and to institute new Government."

Our politicians have caused division amongst Americans, taking away our equality. The leaders in office cannot talk among themselves while conducting business inside the chambers of government. This government has been and is indoctrinating our children. They are being taught how terrible they are while being held down, instead of being held up and told what they can do with hard work and determination.

American history is being destroyed while the government holds onto power. The people need to realize that these politicians work for us, being paid by us, and think we are inferior to them. This is not the equality that is mentioned in our Declaration of Independence.

Politicians have excited Domestic violence between citizens.

This division we talk about continues as both parties have encouraged domestic violence, failing to follow the Rule of Law, or have remained silent when protests erupted across our nation. Violence is in our cities and at the borders, drug abuse, sex abuse, child trafficking, murders, the sectioning of city blocks which were not policed, but aided by our government. History proved that the Taliban had sectioned cities, aiding Afghanistan to fall into the hands of terrorists, causing the attacks on September 11th. The results of this twenty-year war? Afghanistan fell into the hands of the Taliban again. We need to follow the Rule of Law where all citizens, institutions, and community, are accountable for equally enforcing of the law.

Politicians who confuse citizens by passing legislation late at night are representatives that do not take the constituents' interest into account.

The Infrastructure Bill was passed late at night, with a statement, "The bill needs to be passed in order to know what's in it." A bill that has over 2,000 pages, passed late at night appears to be corrupted. Were all House and Senate members invited to conference this bill? Our legislators are not writing these bills, the special interests, and bureaucracy are writing them and benefiting instead of the constituents. No one in Congress could read a bill with over 2,000 pages and comprehend its meaning late at night. A bill should only consist of information that supports it.

Politicians have failed our citizens by imposing taxes without our consent.

This country fought the revolutionary war over a 2 ½ cents tax on a cup of tea, rallying about "no taxation without representation," during the British rule in the 1770s. Here we are today with taxes being imposed on the American people without our consent to pay for social programs, inflation, and hidden taxes. These taxes violate a basic principle of taxation and helps increase the size of the government. The people have given the power to the government with their own interest ahead of the constituents. We left these politicians in office for decades as they became powerful, richer, and corrupt as we continue to struggle for our independence.

Politicians kept a Standing Army in Washington in violation our Constitution.

A standing Army facing outward toward we the people was surrounding the Capitol Building keeping American citizens out. This indicates that this army is to protect the legislators from us, the American people. As we fear our government, it seems our government fears us as well. The administration sees us as their problem, a threat. They fear unity, communities, grassroots, and communication amongst us. Therefore, they embrace division, labeling, separation, giving to some while taking from others. A total lack of policing. The loss of power and money is what they fear most, and the American people can take that away. America needs to be brought back to its history, starting with our politicians.

Politicians have forced businesses to close due to a lack of leadership

Our small businesses had to close their doors and lose generations of hard work and accomplishments. They lived the American dream, and it was taken away. This happed due to the lack of leadership during the war on COVID-19. This war will never end, just like all the previous Wars the government has declared, such as: The War on Drugs, The War on Crime, The War on Terrorism and now The War on COVID-19. Politicians today like to declare war on different subjects to make an impact, and then do nothing to assist with a solution. The Constitution protects the rights and liberties of the citizens from the national government limiting them. Our representatives are not following through on governing by the Constitution, but making up slogans that hurt us, while creating fear so they can control the people.

Politicians have failed to be accountable to each citizen they represent

We do not hold our politicians accountable for their actions. We can all ask ourselves, what an elected official has done that was illegal. The answer would be different throughout generations because it's been an ongoing problem for years. This is unresolved due to a lack of accountability for the American people. They do not hold up their Oath in office and do not respect the Oath taken while questioned on the bench.

Politicians have refused the constituents' demand for term limits.

It was last discussed in the Full House during the Contract with America in 1994. It lost by one vote which was a Republican, this being the party that introduced the bill. Due to this one-vote discrepancy, the Bill should be re-introduced, to help contain the overgrown, powerful, wealthy representatives in office today.

There will always be injustices, and this party will recognize and minimize the severity of such injustices. The candidates of the ICP will report back to its constituents and work with them. This platform is being written to develop a more perfect union along with a more perfect candidate, with God's will and guidance. The time has time come to ***"RESTORE FAITH IN AMERICA."*** With your help we can achieve that. This country is full of political asses and elephants and it's time to be a lion with a loud roar. It's time to hear what people had to say about this topic.

***Bobbie:*** *"I am tired of the dirty political ads, the lies, so called promises etc. I'm tired of the politicians lining their pockets while countless Americans go hungry. I'm tired of their blame games. I want people who are willing to work for the people with truth and integrity."*

***Lorraine:*** *"I would love one party called The American Party. People that care about our country and not themselves. But I am only dreaming. It will never happen." This could happen and will happen if we all come together.*

***Laura:*** *"We were hoping Trump would start a Constitutional Party. He is the only one with the "clout" to do it. I think he has enough people that the RINO GOP and the corrupt D's would be outnumbered by it."*

***David:*** *"That would be nice but at this time and place it would be a disaster, it would split the Republicans and Democrats would hold together ensuring another victory for them, we must not at this juncture cause anything to interfere with a republican election, which I hope is overwhelming! Maybe further down the road it would be great to have a Total Patriot party made up of all races and nationalities to show that it is they not us who are the actual bigots and racist, and with America first policies we will stand United, maybe we can turn the republicans around to being the* *patriots and then we could rename the party without upsetting the apple cart!"*

We cannot worry what will happen to other parties because they have failed us for far too long. We cannot be pessimists we must be optimists, and we never know an outcome until we try and give it our best.

*Marshall:* *"A Democratic Socialist Party"*

*Kerry:* *"The American party. I have found many fear being involved per repercussions."*

*William:* *"I prefer to honor the wisdom of George Washington and consider Party politics of ANY kind, to be a great danger to a Constitutional Republic form of society. Party politics is antithetical to the Constitution and history itself has proven that, ever since the European Elitist element established the Democrat Party in 1828. Just remember that the Nazi Party was/is a political party too."*

*Faith:* *"Constitutional Conservative Party - and hold those who broke their oath of office accountable."*

*Dustin:* *"I would like to see the principles and the party of the Bull Moose to return. It is my firm belief that we must take progressive actions as life moves forward, but also such progressive legislation must be carefully balanced by logic, reason, and testing."*

*Kendall:* *"I would consider a new party. I'm done with the Dems and establishment RINOs"*

*Ryan:* *"Officially switched to Constitution Party last year."*

*Elaine:* *"Already registered as Constitution Part."*

*Julie:* *"How about the Patriot Party?"*

*Terry:* *"I recommend the LARI Party… the Liberal Anti-Republican Independent Party! Committed to vote for whichever candidate has the greatest chance of defeating the Republican candidate!"*

*Karen:* *"We do need more than two parties, but we cannot switch until after the next election or republicans will win it. I like Adam Kinzinger party."*

*James:* *"No…. without term limits I would just have to follow more corrupt, self-serving, egotistical, privileged, wealthy individuals from the intelligence class."*

***Lucky:*** *"I have tried every party and Ross Perot! We need to do away with parties altogether! We need a massive protest in DC….peaceful of course….and include every group with a grievance!! United as Americans!"*

***Brian:*** *"Obviously, there is a great deal of variety within the 70% who would like to see an alternative party. I had been a Republican for 35 years before 2016, but I had been increasingly frustrated, going at least as far back as the Speakership of Newt Gingrich and California Governorship of Pete Wilson. Donald Trump was simply a line I could not cross. But neither could I stomach the Democrats. So, I defined what I wanted to find in a party and went looking for that. I had to search but discovered the American Solidarity Party. With so many people searching, I expect several new parties to spring up, and over the course of time, it will be interesting to see which ones survive and thrive."*

***Martin:*** *"Yes. Republicans are not the answer to the Democrats Fascist ways.*

Just a few observations, and since this was so long, we're just going to hit them all one by one:

1. "Politicians don't work for us anymore " And 46 even admitted this during his 2020 campaign. Remember his argument with the factory worker: "I don't work for you."

2. The American political system works great when it is enforced. Problem is that the courts have become just as corrupt as the political system. For example, the constitution clearly states that only congress can make laws, yet many governmental enforcement agencies, e.g., EPA, ATF, FDA, and FAA, just to name a few, are making laws. EPA has already lost a case because of this, and ATF is about to go down next. Our system isn't broken, it's been highjacked, and we need to take it back. This is what Trump was trying to do. It's why both sides turned on him.

3. "We can't be afraid to get involved…" Seriously? That's what the "Tea Party" movement tried, look what happened to them. Until we get the politics out of law enforcement, we will always be at great risk when going after them.

3a. While it is extremely risky to get involved, I am not saying that people shouldn't do it. I'm just saying that it is disingenuous to tell people that there is no risk, (or imply that there is no or little risk with phrases like that one) because that is an absolute lie, and you should already know that. To give facts in such a way that is intended to lead someone to conclude something that is not correct is lying. Which makes you no better than any other politician or news source who is lying to We the People. Is that what you really want to be associated with?

*Cindy:* "*I would like a party that will speak up for the citizens and not who is paying them.*"

*Vic:* "*One that wrote a creed that the elected members of that actually followed. That they actually work for the people, transparently, not for their campaign funds. That's a start.*"

*Ronin:* "*If a "new" party is developed. To get to Congress and be a majority winning vote party. It would start with winning City Council seats moving to their state house and then into Congress. Would have to establish what it stood for and have an accomplished history. Just can't start at the top. Need allies in Congress etc.*"

*Andrew:* "*Since I'm unaffiliated with either party, it doesn't matter. But a new party would have to concentrate on securing our borders, cutting useless spending, no bailouts for anybody ever, no more money to other countries, lowering all taxes, improving healthcare and education, and above all else, fiercely protecting our Constitutional rights.*"

*Diane:* "*I'm Independent and I'm a Jew who Believes In JESUS. I Wouldn't Change That for Anything.*"

*Patricio:* "*I've never voted mainstream party. 3rd party is the only way to go. Currently I side with libertarians, but all 3rd party groups lack the funding to really be competitive.*"

*Robert:* "*Don't care about parties. Follow the constitution or face a firing squad. Plain and simple.*"

*Melissa:* "*I totally agree. We need term limits and neither side agree with that. That's how they become millionaires and all the while the American people suffer.*"

*David:* "*A Party that pushed for term limits.*"

*Joseph:* "*I would love to see a viable 3rd party that's guaranteed a spot on the stage thru out the election process. Would also like to see a person come out of that as our president.* Me change *parties? I highly doubt it because I don't belong to a political group. I am a true independent voter meaning I can vote for any parties I want. Parties is for politicians not voters. Listen to all vote for the one you like regardless of party affiliation."*

**Chazz:** *"Actually, I did switch political parties. I was a lifelong Democrat I was a republican for about a week and now I'm an independent. Most people are middle of the road, and you can't put them in boxes by column just liberal or conservative. I'm a moderate I'm in the middle. I just say no more Trump no more left extreme climate cult religiousness & the end of wokeness in politics and our society which they are ruining."*

There you have it; people are fed up with the two-party system and want change. Not everyone, but more than we thought. We realize we will not change everyone's mind of getting involved with a new party. We are not a third party; we are a minor party that will be the big brother in all political rooms. Look us up on Facebook at the United States Constitutional Group at httt://fedupwithpolitics.com and the link to get on our Independent Constitutional Party webpage will be on that. You can also view our weekly show and hear directly where we believe this country is heading thanks to lackluster politicians. Our apple podcast is the Jack and Dennis show and find us on YouTube at Stand United with Jack and Dennis. We will leave you on one last quote and here it, is by

**Trent:** *"The problem we are in is we are damned if do and damned if we don't. If we don't have a new party that is truly about the constitution and the citizens of this country, I'm afraid this country as we know it will fail. But if we don't support the Republicans now the Democrats will completely and utterly destroy the few freedoms, we do still have.... It truly is a sad state of affairs."*

# Conclusion

And that my friends, is the completion of our book, by the people, for the people. We again appreciate everyone who took the time to comment on our questions. This edition would never have been completed without you, our Facebook friends. Our only wish is that these politicians elected to city, state, and federal office will read it and finally understand what the people feel about important issues in the United States.

There will always be topics to read about and always another opportunity for your involvement. These are just our starting points to ease into what we need fixed in this great country. Our country is not what it used to be, and we are the only ones who can fix it.

Be that **PATRIOT** to get involved and help each other win back our government. Stop relying on news media outlets to get your information, get out of that house. Even though we have lower COVID numbers, if you feel you still need Personal Protective Equipment (PPE), wear it. Attend church functions, join a Moose Club, or attend those sports games we all like to go to, that is where you find out what is happening in your community. Join political clubs if you are angry about everything you see and hear. Talk to your neighbor; you will find most of them have the same concerns as you, and even if they have a difference of opinion, it does not mean they are wrong. If you feel they are wrong, debate them in an honest way without getting annoyed. Be that one person where others come to you and ask your advice. Remember that we all have opinions, so we must do our due diligence and research the topic to be the most informed person in the room. Don't believe what others have said until you verify. If you want to be involved in any future books, email us at uscg20211@aol.com and we will be more than happy to add you to our already-growing list. The more you know, the more you grow, and less people can take advantage of you. We are counting on you, our Patriot brothers, and sisters from all walks of life, to help us achieve our grassroots mission. When we do our show, we always say these three words—please take these words wisely, since they are extremely important. We look forward to hearing from you in the future because "KNOWLEDGE IS POWER."

# Our Forefathers' Plan

## *Declaration of Independence*
In Congress, July 4, 1776

"The unanimous Declaration of the thirteen united States of America, When in the Course of human events, it becomes necessary for one people to dissolve the political bands which have connected them with another, and to assume among the powers of the earth, the separate and equal station to which the Laws of Nature and of Nature's God entitle them, a decent respect to the opinions of mankind requires that they should declare the causes which impel them to the separation.

We hold these truths to be self-evident, that all men are created equal, that they are endowed by their Creator with certain unalienable Rights, that among these are Life, Liberty and the pursuit of Happiness.—That to secure these rights, Governments are instituted among Men, deriving their just powers from the consent of the governed, —That whenever any Form of Government becomes destructive of these ends, it is the Right of the People to alter or to abolish it, and to institute new Government, laying its foundation on such principles and organizing its powers in such form, as to them shall seem most likely to effect their Safety and Happiness. Prudence, indeed, will dictate that Governments long established should not be changed for light and transient causes; and accordingly, all experience hath shewn, that mankind are more disposed to suffer, while evils are sufferable, than to right themselves by abolishing the forms to which they are accustomed. But when a long train of abuses and usurpations, pursuing invariably the same Object evinces a design to reduce them under absolute Despotism, it is their right, it is their duty, to throw off such Government, and to provide new Guards for their future security.—Such has been the patient sufferance of these Colonies; and such is now the necessity which constrains them to alter their former Systems of Government. The history of the present King of Great Britain is a history of repeated injuries and usurpations, all having in direct object the establishment of an absolute Tyranny over these States. To prove this, let Facts be submitted to a candid world.

He has refused his Assent to Laws, the most wholesome and necessary for the public good.

He has forbidden his Governors to pass Laws of immediate and pressing importance, unless suspended in their operation till his Assent should be obtained; and when so suspended, he has utterly neglected to attend to them.

He has refused to pass other Laws for the accommodation of large districts of people, unless those people would relinquish the right of Representation in the Legislature, a right inestimable to them and formidable to tyrants only.

He has called together legislative bodies at places unusual, uncomfortable, and distant from the depository of their public Records, for the sole purpose of fatiguing them into compliance with his measures.

He has dissolved Representative Houses repeatedly, for opposing with manly firmness his invasions on the rights of the people.

He has refused for a long time, after such dissolutions, to cause others to be elected; whereby the Legislative powers, incapable of Annihilation, have returned to the People at large for their exercise; the State remaining in the meantime exposed to all the dangers of invasion from without, and convulsions within.

He has endeavored to prevent the population of these States; for that purpose, obstructing the Laws for Naturalization of Foreigners; refusing to pass others to encourage their migrations hither, and raising the conditions of new Appropriations of Lands.

He has obstructed the Administration of Justice, by refusing his Assent to Laws for establishing Judiciary powers.

He has made Judges dependent on his Will alone, for the tenure of their offices, and the amount and payment of their salaries."

He has erected a multitude of New Offices and sent hither swarms of Officers to harass our people, and eat out their substance.

He has kept among us, in times of peace, Standing Armies without the Consent of our legislatures.

He has affected to render the Military independent of and superior to the Civil power.

He has combined with others to subject us to a jurisdiction foreign to our constitution, and unacknowledged by our laws, giving his Assent to their Acts of pretended Legislation:

For Quartering large bodies of armed troops among us:

For protecting them, by a mock Trial, from punishment for any Murders which they should commit on the Inhabitants of these States:

For cutting off our Trade with all parts of the world:

For imposing Taxes on us without our Consent:

For depriving us in many cases, of the benefits of Trial by Jury:

For transporting us beyond Seas to be tried for pretended offences

For abolishing the free System of English Laws in a neighboring Province, establishing therein an Arbitrary government, and enlarging its Boundaries so as to render it at once an example and fit instrument for introducing the same absolute rule into these Colonies:

For taking away our Charters, abolishing our most valuable Laws, and altering fundamentally the Forms of our Governments:

For suspending our own Legislatures, and declaring themselves invested with power to legislate for us in all cases whatsoever.

He has abdicated Government here, by declaring us out of his Protection and waging War against us.

He has plundered our seas, ravaged our Coasts, burnt our towns, and destroyed the lives of our people.

He is at this time transporting large Armies of foreign Mercenaries to complete the works of death, desolation, and tyranny, already begun with circumstances of Cruelty & perfidy scarcely paralleled in the most barbarous ages, and totally unworthy the Head of a civilized nation.

He has constrained our fellow Citizens taken Captive on the high Seas to bear Arms against their Country, to become the executioners of their friends and Brethren, or to fall themselves by their Hands.

He has excited domestic insurrections amongst us, and has endeavored to bring on the inhabitants of our frontiers, the merciless Indian Savages, whose known rule of warfare, is an undistinguished destruction of all ages, sexes and conditions.

In every stage of these Oppressions We have Petitioned for Redress in the most humble terms: Our repeated Petitions have been answered only by repeated injury. A Prince whose character is thus marked by every act which may define a Tyrant, is unfit to be the ruler of a free people.

Nor have We been wanting in attentions to our Brattish brethren. We have warned them from time to time of attempts by their legislature to extend an unwarrantable jurisdiction over us. We have reminded them of the circumstances of our emigration and settlement here. We have appealed to their native justice and magnanimity, and we have conjured them by the ties of our common kindred to disavow these usurpations, which, would inevitably interrupt our connections and correspondence. They too have been deaf to the voice of justice and of consanguinity. We must, therefore, acquiesce in the necessity, which denounces our Separation, and hold them, as we hold the rest of mankind, Enemies in War, in Peace Friends.

We, therefore, the Representatives of the united States of America, in General Congress, Assembled, appealing to the Supreme Judge of the world for the rectitude of our intentions, do, in the Name, and by Authority of the good People of these Colonies, solemnly publish and declare, That these United Colonies are, and of Right ought to be Free and Independent States; that they are Absolved from all Allegiance to the British Crown, and that all political connection between them and the State of Great Britain, is and ought to be totally dissolved; and that as Free and Independent States, they have full Power to levy War, conclude Peace, contract Alliances, establish Commerce, and to do all other Acts and Things which Independent States may of right do. And for the support of this Declaration, with a firm reliance on the protection of divine Providence, we mutually pledge to each other our Lives, our Fortunes and our sacred Honor.

# The United States Constitution

**Preamble**

We the People of the United States, in Order to form a more perfect Union, establish Justice, insure domestic Tranquility, provide for the common defense, promote the general Welfare, and secure the Blessings of Liberty to ourselves and our Posterity, do ordain and establish this Constitution for the United States of America.

## Article I

**Section I**

All legislative Powers herein granted shall be vested in a Congress of the United States, which shall consist of a Senate and House of Representatives.

**Section 2**

The House of Representatives shall be composed of Members chosen every second Year by the People of the several States, and the Electors in each State shall have the Qualifications requisite for Electors of the most numerous Branch of the State Legislature.

No Person shall be a Representative who shall not have attained to the Age of twenty-five Years, and been seven Years a Citizen of the United States, and who shall not, when elected, be an Inhabitant of that State in which he shall be chosen.

Representatives and direct Taxes shall be apportioned among the several States which may be included within this Union, according to their respective Numbers, which shall be determined by adding to the whole Number of free Persons, including those bound to Service for a Term of Years, and excluding Indians not taxed, three fifths of all other Persons. The actual Enumeration shall be made within three Years after the first Meeting of the Congress of the United States, and within every subsequent Term of ten Years, in such Manner as they shall by Law direct. The Number of Representatives shall not exceed one for every thirty Thousand, but each State shall have at Least one Representative; and until such enumeration shall be made, the State of New Hampshire shall be entitled to chuse three, Massachusetts eight, Rhode-Island and Providence Plantations one, Connecticut five, New-York six, New Jersey four, Pennsylvania eight, Delaware one, Maryland six, Virginia ten, North Carolina five, South Carolina five, and Georgia three.

When vacancies happen in the Representation from any State, the Executive Authority thereof shall issue Writs of Election to fill such Vacancies.

The House of Representatives shall chuse their Speaker and other Officers; and shall have the sole Power of Impeachment.

## Section 3

The Senate of the United States shall be composed of two Senators from each State, chosen by the Legislature thereof, for six Years; and each Senator shall have one Vote.

Immediately after they shall be assembled in Consequence of the first Election, they shall be divided as equally as may be into three Classes. The Seats of the Senators of the first Class shall be vacated at the Expiration of the second Year, of the second Class at the Expiration of the fourth Year, and of the third Class at the Expiration of the sixth Year, so that one third may be chosen every second Year; and if Vacancies happen by Resignation, or otherwise, during the Recess of the Legislature of any State, the Executive thereof may make temporary Appointments until the next Meeting of the Legislature, which shall then fill such Vacancies.

No Person shall be a Senator who shall not have attained to the Age of thirty Years, and been nine Years a Citizen of the United States, and who shall not, when elected, be an Inhabitant of that State for which he shall be chosen.

The Vice President of the United States shall be President of the Senate, but shall have no Vote, unless they be equally divided.

The Senate shall chuse their other Officers, and also a President pro tempore, in the Absence of the Vice President, or when he shall exercise the Office of President of the United States.

The Senate shall have the sole Power to try all Impeachments. When sitting for that Purpose, they shall be on Oath or Affirmation. When the President of the United States is tried, the Chief Justice shall preside: And no Person shall be convicted without the Concurrence of two thirds of the Members present.

Judgment in Cases of Impeachment shall not extend further than to removal from Office, and disqualification to hold and enjoy any Office of honor, Trust or Profit under the United States: but the Party convicted shall nevertheless be liable and subject to Indictment, Trial, Judgment and Punishment, according to Law.

## Section 4

The Times, Places and Manner of holding Elections for Senators and Representatives, shall be prescribed in each State by the Legislature thereof; but the Congress may at any time by Law make or alter such Regulations, except as to the Places of chusing Senators.

The Congress shall assemble at least once in every Year, and such Meeting shall be on the first Monday in December, unless they shall by Law appoint a different Day.

## Section 5

Each House shall be the Judge of the Elections, Returns and Qualifications of its own Members, and a Majority of each shall constitute a Quorum to do Business; but a smaller Number may adjourn from day to day, and may be authorized to compel the Attendance of absent Members, in such Manner, and under such Penalties as each House may provide.

Each House may determine the Rules of its Proceedings, punish its Members for disorderly Behaviour, and, with the Concurrence of two thirds, expel a Member.

Each House shall keep a Journal of its Proceedings, and from time to time publish the same, excepting such Parts as may in their Judgment require Secrecy; and the Yeas and Nays of the Members of either House on any question shall, at the Desire of one fifth of those Present, be entered on the Journal.

Neither House, during the Session of Congress, shall, without the Consent of the other, adjourn for more than three days, nor to any other Place than that in which the two Houses shall be sitting.

## Section 6

The Senators and Representatives shall receive a Compensation for their Services, to be ascertained by Law, and paid out of the Treasury of the United

States. They shall in all Cases, except Treason, Felony and Breach of the Peace, be privileged from Arrest during their Attendance at the Session of their respective Houses, and in going to and returning from the same; and for any Speech or Debate in either House, they shall not be questioned in any other Place.

No Senator or Representative shall, during the Time for which he was elected, be appointed to any civil Office under the Authority of the United States, which shall have been created, or the Emoluments whereof shall have been encreased during such time; and no Person holding any Office under the United States, shall be a Member of either House during his Continuance in Office.

## Section 7

All Bills for raising Revenue shall originate in the House of Representatives; but the Senate may propose or concur with Amendments as on other Bills.

Every Bill which shall have passed the House of Representatives and the Senate, shall, before it become a Law, be presented to the President of the United States: If he approve he shall sign it, but if not he shall return it, with his Objections to that House in which it shall have originated, who shall enter the Objections at large on their Journal, and proceed to reconsider it. If after such Reconsideration two thirds of that House shall agree to pass the Bill, it shall be sent, together with the Objections, to the other House, by which it shall likewise be reconsidered, and if approved by two thirds of that House, it shall become a Law. But in all such Cases the Votes of both Houses shall be determined by Yeas and Nays, and the Names of the Persons voting for and against the Bill shall be entered on the Journal of each House respectively. If any Bill shall not be returned by the President within ten Days (Sundays excepted) after it shall have been presented to him, the Same shall be a Law, in like Manner as if he had signed it, unless the Congress by their Adjournment prevent its Return, in which Case it shall not be a Law.

Every Order, Resolution, or Vote to which the Concurrence of the Senate and House of Representatives may be necessary (except on a question of Adjournment) shall be presented to the President of the United States; and before the Same shall take Effect, shall be approved by him, or being disapproved by him, shall be repassed by two thirds of the Senate and House of Representatives, according to the Rules and Limitations prescribed in the Case of a Bill.

**Section 8**

The Congress shall have Power To lay and collect Taxes, Duties, Imposts and Excises, to pay the Debts and provide for the common Defence and general Welfare of the United States; but all Duties, Imposts and Excises shall be uniform throughout the United States;

To borrow Money on the credit of the United States;

To regulate Commerce with foreign Nations, and among the several States, and with the Indian Tribes;

To establish an uniform Rule of Naturalization, and uniform Laws on the subject of Bankruptcies throughout the United States;

To coin Money, regulate the Value thereof, and of foreign Coin, and fix the Standard of Weights and Measures;

To provide for the Punishment of counterfeiting the Securities and current Coin of the United States;

To establish Post Offices and post Roads;

To promote the Progress of Science and useful Arts, by securing for limited Times to Authors and Inventors the exclusive Right to their respective Writings and Discoveries;

To constitute Tribunals inferior to the supreme Court;

To define and punish Piracies and Felonies committed on the high Seas, and Offences against the Law of Nations;

To declare War, grant Letters of Marque and Reprisal, and make Rules concerning Captures on Land and Water;

To raise and support Armies, but no Appropriation of Money to that Use shall be for a longer Term than two Years;

To provide and maintain a Navy;

To make Rules for the Government and Regulation of the land and naval Forces;

To provide for calling forth the Militia to execute the Laws of the Union, suppress Insurrections and repel Invasions;

To provide for organizing, arming, and disciplining, the Militia, and for governing such Part of them as may be employed in the Service of the United States, reserving to the States respectively, the Appointment of the Officers, and the Authority of training the Militia according to the discipline prescribed by Congress;

To exercise exclusive Legislation in all Cases whatsoever, over such District (not exceeding ten Miles square) as may, by Cession of particular States, and the Acceptance of Congress, become the Seat of the Government of the United States, and to exercise like Authority over all Places purchased by the Consent of the Legislature of the State in which the Same shall be, for the Erection of Forts, Magazines, Arsenals, dock-Yards, and other needful Buildings;—And

To make all Laws which shall be necessary and proper for carrying into Execution the foregoing Powers, and all other Powers vested by this Constitution in the Government of the United States, or in any Department or Officer thereof.

## Section 9

The Migration or Importation of such Persons as any of the States now existing shall think proper to admit, shall not be prohibited by the Congress prior to the Year one thousand eight hundred and eight, but a Tax or duty may be imposed on such Importation, not exceeding ten dollars for each Person.

The Privilege of the Writ of Habeas Corpus shall not be suspended, unless when in Cases of Rebellion or Invasion the public Safety may require it.

No Bill of Attainder or ex post facto Law shall be passed.

No Capitation, or other direct, Tax shall be laid, unless in Proportion to the Census or enumeration herein before directed to be taken.

No Tax or Duty shall be laid on Articles exported from any State.

No Preference shall be given by any Regulation of Commerce or Revenue to the Ports of one State over those of another; nor shall Vessels bound to, or from, one State, be obliged to enter, clear, or pay Duties in another.

No Money shall be drawn from the Treasury, but in Consequence of Appropriations made by Law; and a regular Statement and Account of the Receipts and Expenditures of all public Money shall be published from time to time.

No Title of Nobility shall be granted by the United States: And no Person holding any Office of Profit or Trust under them, shall, without the Consent of the Congress, accept of any present, Emolument, Office, or Title, of any kind whatever, from any King, Prince, or foreign State.

**Section 10**

No State shall enter into any Treaty, Alliance, or Confederation; grant Letters of Marque and Reprisal; coin Money; emit Bills of Credit; make any Thing but gold and silver Coin a Tender in Payment of Debts; pass any Bill of Attainder, ex post facto Law, or Law impairing the Obligation of Contracts, or grant any Title of Nobility.

No State shall, without the Consent of the Congress, lay any Imposts or Duties on Imports or Exports, except what may be absolutely necessary for executing its inspection Laws: and the net Produce of all Duties and Imposts, laid by any State on Imports or Exports, shall be for the Use of the Treasury of the United States; and all such Laws shall be subject to the Revision and Control of the Congress.

No State shall, without the Consent of Congress, lay any Duty of Tonnage, keep Troops, or Ships of War in time of Peace, enter into any Agreement or Compact with another State, or with a foreign Power, or engage in War, unless actually invaded, or in such imminent Danger as will not admit of delay.

## Article II

**Section 1**

The executive Power shall be vested in a President of the United States of America. He shall hold his Office during the Term of four Years, and, together with the Vice President, chosen for the same Term, be elected, as follows:

Each State shall appoint, in such Manner as the Legislature thereof may direct, a Number of Electors, equal to the whole Number of Senators and Representatives to which the State may be entitled in the Congress: but no Senator or Representative, or Person holding an Office of Trust or Profit under the United States, shall be appointed an Elector.

The Electors shall meet in their respective States, and vote by Ballot for two Persons, of whom one at least shall not be an Inhabitant of the same State with themselves. And they shall make a List of all the Persons voted for, and of the Number of Votes for each; which List they shall sign and certify, and transmit sealed to the Seat of the Government of the United States, directed to the President of the Senate. The President of the Senate shall, in the Presence of the Senate and House of Representatives, open all the Certificates, and the Votes shall then be counted. The Person having the greatest Number of Votes shall be the President, if such Number be a Majority of the whole Number of Electors appointed; and if there be more than one who have such Majority, and have an equal Number of Votes, then the House of Representatives shall immediately choose by Ballot one of them for President; and if no Person have a Majority, then from the five highest on the List the said House shall in like Manner choose the President. But in chusing the President, the Votes shall be taken by States, the Representatives from each State having one Vote; a quorum for this Purpose shall consist of a Member or Members from two thirds of the States, and a Majority of all the States shall be necessary to a Choice. In every Case, after the Choice of the President, the Person having the greatest Number of Votes of the Electors shall be the Vice President. But if there should remain two or more who have equal Votes, the Senate shall choose from them by Ballot the Vice-President.

The Congress may determine the Time of choosing the Electors, and the Day on which they shall give their Votes; which Day shall be the same throughout the United States.

No Person except a natural born Citizen, or a Citizen of the United States, at the time of the Adoption of this Constitution, shall be eligible to the Office of President; neither shall any person be eligible to that Office who shall not have attained to the Age of thirty five Years, and been fourteen Years a Resident within the United States.

In Case of the Removal of the President from Office, or of his Death, Resignation, or Inability to discharge the Powers and Duties of the said Office, the Same shall devolve on the Vice President, and the Congress may by Law provide for the Case of Removal, Death, Resignation or Inability, both of the President and Vice President, declaring what Officer shall then act as President, and such Officer shall act accordingly, until the Disability be removed, or a President shall be elected.

The President shall, at stated Times, receive for his Services, a Compensation, which shall neither be encreased nor diminished during the Period for which he shall have been elected, and he shall not receive within that Period any other Emolument from the United States, or any of them.

Before he enter on the Execution of his Office, he shall take the following Oath or Affirmation: —"I do solemnly swear (or affirm) that I will faithfully execute the Office of President of the United States, and will to the best of my Ability, preserve, protect and defend the Constitution of the United States."

## Section 2

The President shall be Commander in Chief of the Army and Navy of the United States, and of the Militia of the several States, when called into the actual Service of the United States; he may require the Opinion, in writing, of the principal Officer in each of the executive Departments, upon any Subject relating to the Duties of their respective Offices, and he shall have Power to Grant Reprieves and Pardons for Offences against the United States, except in Cases of Impeachment.

He shall have Power, by and with the Advice and Consent of the Senate, to make Treaties, provided two thirds of the Senators present concur; and he shall nominate, and by and with the Advice and Consent of the Senate, shall appoint Ambassadors, other public Ministers and Consuls, Judges of the supreme Court, and all other Officers of the United States, whose Appointments are not herein otherwise provided for, and which shall be established by Law: but the Congress may by Law vest the Appointment of such inferior Officers, as they think proper, in the President alone, in the Courts of Law, or in the Heads of Departments.

The President shall have Power to fill up all Vacancies that may happen during the Recess of the Senate, by granting Commissions which shall expire at the End of their next Session.

## Section 3

He shall from time to time give to the Congress Information of the State of the Union, and recommend to their Consideration such Measures as he shall judge necessary and expedient; he may, on extraordinary Occasions, convene both Houses, or either of them, and in Case of Disagreement between them, with Respect to the Time of Adjournment, he may adjourn them to such Time as he shall think proper; he shall receive Ambassadors and other public Ministers; he shall take Care that the Laws be faithfully executed, and shall Commission all the Officers of the United States.

## Section 4

The President, Vice President and all Civil Officers of the United States, shall be removed from Office on Impeachment for, and Conviction of, Treason, Bribery, or other high Crimes and Misdemeanors.

## Article III

## Section 1

The judicial Power of the United States, shall be vested in one supreme Court, and in such inferior Courts as the Congress may from time to time ordain and establish. The Judges, both of the supreme and inferior Courts, shall hold their Offices during good Behaviour, and shall, at stated Times, receive for their Services, a Compensation, which shall not be diminished during their Continuance in Office.

## Section 2

The judicial Power shall extend to all Cases, in Law and Equity, arising under this Constitution, the Laws of the United States, and Treaties made, or which shall be made, under their Authority;—to all Cases affecting Ambassadors, other public ministers and Consuls;—to all Cases of admiralty and maritime Jurisdiction;—to Controversies to which the United States shall be a Party;—to Controversies between two or more States;—between a State and Citizens of another State;—between Citizens of different States;—between Citizens of the same State claiming Lands under Grants of different States, and between a State, or the Citizens thereof, and foreign States, Citizens or Subjects.

In all Cases affecting Ambassadors, other public Ministers and Consuls, and those in which a State shall be Party, the supreme Court shall have original Jurisdiction. In all the other Cases before mentioned, the supreme Court shall have appellate Jurisdiction, both as to Law and Fact, with such Exceptions, and under such Regulations as the Congress shall make.

The Trial of all Crimes, except in Cases of Impeachment, shall be by Jury; and such Trial shall be held in the State where the said Crimes shall have been committed; but when not committed within any State, the Trial shall be at such Place or Places as the Congress may by Law have directed.

## Section 3

Treason against the United States, shall consist only in levying War against them, or in adhering to their Enemies, giving them Aid and Comfort. No Person shall be convicted of Treason unless on the Testimony of two Witnesses to the same overt Act, or on Confession in open Court.

The Congress shall have Power to declare the Punishment of Treason, but no Attainder of Treason shall work Corruption of Blood, or Forfeiture except during the Life of the Person attainted.

## Article IV

## Section 1

Full Faith and Credit shall be given in each State to the public Acts, Records, and judicial Proceedings of every other State. And the Congress may by general Laws prescribe the Manner in which such Acts, Records and Proceedings shall be proved, and the Effect thereof.

## Section 2

The Citizens of each State shall be entitled to all Privileges and Immunities of Citizens in the several States.

A Person charged in any State with Treason, Felony, or other Crime, who shall flee from Justice, and be found in another State, shall on Demand of the executive Authority of the State from which he fled, be delivered up, to be removed to the State having Jurisdiction of the Crime

No Person held to Service or Labour in one State, under the Laws thereof, escaping into another, shall, in Consequence of any Law or Regulation therein, be discharged from such Service or Labour, but shall be delivered up on Claim of the Party to whom such Service or Labour may be due.

## Section 3

New States may be admitted by the Congress into this Union; but no new State shall be formed or erected within the Jurisdiction of any other State; nor any State be formed by the Junction of two or more States, or Parts of

States, without the Consent of the Legislatures of the States concerned as well as of the Congress.

The Congress shall have Power to dispose of and make all needful Rules and Regulations respecting the Territory or other Property belonging to the United States; and nothing in this Constitution shall be so construed as to Prejudice any Claims of the United States, or of any particular State.

**Section 4**

The United States shall guarantee to every State in this Union a Republican Form of Government, and shall protect each of them against Invasion; and on Application of the Legislature, or of the Executive (when the Legislature cannot be convened) against domestic Violence.

## Article V

The Congress, whenever two thirds of both Houses shall deem it necessary, shall propose Amendments to this Constitution, or, on the Application of the Legislatures of two thirds of the several States, shall call a Convention for proposing Amendments, which, in either Case, shall be valid to all Intents and Purposes, as Part of this Constitution, when ratified by the Legislatures of three fourths of the several States, or by Conventions in three fourths thereof, as the one or the other Mode of Ratification may be proposed by the Congress; Provided that no Amendment which may be made prior to the Year One thousand eight hundred and eight shall in any Manner affect the first and fourth Clauses in the Ninth Section of the first Article; and that no State, without its Consent, shall be deprived of its equal Suffrage in the Senate.

## Article VI

All Debts contracted and Engagements entered into, before the Adoption of this Constitution, shall be as valid against the United States under this Constitution, as under the Confederation

This Constitution, and the Laws of the United States which shall be made in Pursuance thereof; and all Treaties made, or which shall be made, under the Authority of the United States, shall be the supreme Law of the Land; and the

Judges in every State shall be bound thereby, any Thing in the Constitution or Laws of any state to the Contrary notwithstanding.

The Senators and Representatives before mentioned, and the Members of the several State Legislatures, and all executive and judicial Officers, both of the United States and of the several States, shall be bound by Oath or Affirmation, to support this Constitution; but no religious Test shall ever be required as a Qualification to any Office or public Trust under the United States.

## Article VII

The Ratification of the Conventions of nine States, shall be sufficient for the Establishment of this Constitution between the States so ratifying the Same.

Done in Convention by the Unanimous Consent of the States present the Seventeenth Day of September in the Year of our Lord one thousand seven hundred and Eighty seven and of the Independence of the United States of America the Twelfth In Witness whereof We have hereunto subscribed our Names,

George Washington,  President
And deputy from Virginia
New HampshireJohn Langdon
Nicholas Gilman
Massachusetts Nathaniel Gorham
Rufus King
Connecticut Wm. Saml. Johnson
Roger Sherman
New York Alexander Hamilton
New Jersey Wil: Livingston
David Brearley
Wm. Paterson
Jona. Dayton
Pennsylvania B Franklin
Thomas Mifflin
Robt Morris
Geo. Clymer
Thos. FitzSimons

Jared Ingersoll
James Wilson
Gouv Morris
Delaware Geo: Read
Gunning Bedford jun
John Dickinson
Richard Bassett
Jaco: Broom
Maryland James McHenry
Dan of St. Thos. Jenifer
Danl Carroll
VirginiaJohn Blair—
James Madison Jr.
North Carolina Wm. Blount
Richd. Dobbs Spaight
Hu Williamson
South Carolina J. Rutledge
Charles Cotesworth Pinckney
Charles Pinckney
Pierce Butler
Georgia William Few
Abr Baldwin
Attest William Jackson Secretary

## Amendment I (1791)

Congress shall make no law respecting an establishment of religion, or prohibiting the free exercise thereof; or abridging the freedom of speech, or of the press; or the right of the people peaceably to assemble, and to petition the Government for a redress of grievances.

## Amendment II (1791)

A well regulated Militia, being necessary to the security of a free State, the right of the people to keep and bear Arms, shall not be infringed.

### **Amendment III** (1791)

No Soldier shall, in time of peace be quartered in any house, without the consent of the Owner, nor in time of war, but in a manner to be prescribed by law.

### **Amendment IV** (1791)

The right of the people to be secure in their persons, houses, papers, and effects, against unreasonable searches and seizures, shall not be violated, and no Warrants shall issue, but upon probable cause, supported by Oath or affirmation, and particularly describing the place to be searched, and the persons or things to be seized.

### **Amendment V** (1791)

No person shall be held to answer for a capital, or otherwise infamous crime, unless on a presentment or indictment of a Grand Jury, except in cases arising in the land or naval forces, or in the Militia, when in actual service in time of War or public danger; nor shall any person be subject for the same offence to be twice put in jeopardy of life or limb; nor shall be compelled in any criminal case to be a witness against himself, nor be deprived of life, liberty, or property, without due process of law; nor shall private property be taken for public use, without just compensation.

### **Amendment VI** (1791)

In all criminal prosecutions, the accused shall enjoy the right to a speedy and public trial, by an impartial jury of the State and district wherein the crime shall have been committed, which district shall have been previously ascertained by law, and to be informed of the nature and cause of the accusation; to be confronted with the witnesses against him; to have compulsory process for obtaining witnesses in his favor, and to have the Assistance of Counsel for his defence.

### **Amendment VII** (1791)

In Suits at common law, where the value in controversy shall exceed twenty dollars, the right of trial by jury shall be preserved, and no fact tried by a jury, shall be otherwise re-examined in any Court of the United States, than according to the rules of the common law.

### Amendment VIII (1791)

Excessive bail shall not be required, nor excessive fines imposed, nor cruel and unusual punishments inflicted.

### Amendment IX (1791)

The enumeration in the Constitution, of certain rights, shall not be construed to deny or disparage others retained by the people.

### Amendment X (1791)

The powers not delegated to the United States by the Constitution, nor prohibited by it to the States, are reserved to the States respectively, or to the people.

### Amendment XI (1795/1798)

The Judicial power of the United States shall not be construed to extend to any suit in law or equity, commenced or prosecuted against one of the United States by Citizens of another State, or by Citizens or Subjects of any Foreign State.

### Amendment XII (1804)

The Electors shall meet in their respective states and vote by ballot for President and Vice-President, one of whom, at least, shall not be an inhabitant of the same state with themselves; they shall name in their ballots the person voted for as President, and in distinct ballots the person voted for as Vice-President, and they shall make distinct lists of all persons voted for as President, and of all persons voted for as Vice-President, and of the number of votes for each, which lists they shall sign and certify, and transmit sealed to the seat of the government of the United States, directed to the President of the Senate;—The President of the Senate shall, in the presence of the Senate and House of Representatives, open all the certificates and the votes shall then be counted;—The person having the greatest Number of votes for President, shall be the President, if such number be a majority of the whole number of Electors appointed; and if no person have such majority, then from the persons having the highest numbers not exceeding three on the list of those voted for as President, the House of Representatives shall choose immediately, by ballot, the President. But in choosing the President, the votes shall be taken by states, the representation from each state having one vote; a quorum for this purpose shall consist of a member or members from two-thirds of the states, and a majority of all the states shall be necessary to a choice. And if the House of Representatives shall not choose a President whenever the right of choice shall devolve upon them, before the fourth day of March next following, then the Vice-President shall act as President, as in the case of the death or other constitutional disability of the President—The person having the greatest number of votes as Vice-President, shall be the Vice-President, if such number be a majority of the whole number of Electors appointed, and if no person have a majority, then from the two highest numbers on the list, the Senate shall choose the Vice-President; a quorum for the purpose shall consist of two-thirds of the whole number of Senators, and a majority of the whole number shall be necessary to a choice. But no person constitutionally ineligible to the office of President shall be eligible to that of Vice-President of the United States.

## Amendment XIII (1865)

### Section 1

Neither slavery nor involuntary servitude, except as a punishment for crime whereof the party shall have been duly convicted, shall exist within the United States, or any place subject to their jurisdiction.

### Section 2

Congress shall have power to enforce this article by appropriate legislation.

## Amendment XIV (1868)

### Section 1

All persons born or naturalized in the United States, and subject to the jurisdiction thereof, are citizens of the United States and of the State wherein they reside. No State shall make or enforce any law which shall abridge the privileges or immunities of citizens of the United States; nor shall any State deprive any person of life, liberty, or property, without due process of law; nor deny to any person within its jurisdiction the equal protection of the laws.

**Section 2**

Representatives shall be apportioned among the several States according to their respective numbers, counting the whole number of persons in each State, excluding Indians not taxed. But when the right to vote at any election for the choice of electors for President and Vice President of the United States, Representatives in Congress, the Executive and Judicial officers of a State, or the members of the Legislature thereof, is denied to any of the male inhabitants of such State, being twenty-one years of age, and citizens of the United States, or in any way abridged, except for participation in rebellion, or other crime, the basis of representation therein shall be reduced in the proportion which the number of such male citizens shall bear to the whole number of male citizens twenty-one years of age in such State.

**Section 3**

No person shall be a Senator or Representative in Congress, or elector of President and Vice President, or hold any office, civil or military, under the United States, or under any State, who, having previously taken an oath, as a member of Congress, or as an officer of the United States, or as a member of any State legislature, or as an executive or judicial officer of any State, to support the Constitution of the United States, shall have engaged in insurrection or rebellion against the same, or given aid or comfort to the enemies thereof. But Congress may by a vote of two-thirds of each House, remove such disability.

**Section 4**

The validity of the public debt of the United States, authorized by law, including debts incurred for payment of pensions and bounties for services in suppressing insurrection or rebellion, shall not be questioned. But neither the United States nor any State shall assume or pay any debt or obligation incurred in aid of insurrection or rebellion against the United States, or any claim for the loss or emancipation of any slave; but all such debts, obligations and claims shall be held illegal and void.

**Section 5**

The Congress shall have power to enforce, by appropriate legislation, the provisions of this article.

## Amendment XV (1870)

**Section 1**

The right of citizens of the United States to vote shall not be denied or abridged by the United States or by any State on account of race, color, or previous condition of servitude.

**Section 2**

The Congress shall have power to enforce this article by appropriate legislation.

## Amendment XVI (1913)

The Congress shall have power to lay and collect taxes on incomes, from whatever source derived, without apportionment among the several States, and without regard to any census or enumeration.

## Amendment XVII (1913)

The Senate of the United States shall be composed of two Senators from each State, elected by the people thereof, for six years; and each Senator shall have one vote. The electors in each State shall have the qualifications requisite for electors of the most numerous branch of the State legislatures.

When vacancies happen in the representation of any State in the Senate, the executive authority of such State shall issue writs of election to fill such vacancies: Provided, That the legislature of any State may empower the executive thereof to make temporary appointments until the people fill the vacancies by election as the legislature may direct.

This amendment shall not be so construed as to affect the election or term of any Senator chosen before it becomes valid as part of the Constitution.

## Amendment XVIII (1919)

### Section 1

After one year from the ratification of this article the manufacture, sale, or transportation of intoxicating liquors within, the importation thereof into, or the exportation thereof from the United States and all territory subject to the jurisdiction thereof for beverage purposes is hereby prohibited.

### Section 2

The Congress and the several States shall have concurrent power to enforce this article by appropriate legislation.

### Section 3

This article shall be inoperative unless it shall have been ratified as an amendment to the Constitution by the legislatures of the several States, as provided in the Constitution, within seven years from the date of the submission hereof to the States by the Congress.

## Amendment XIX (1920)

The right of citizens of the United States to vote shall not be denied or abridged by the United States or by any State on account of sex.

Congress shall have power to enforce this article by appropriate legislation.

## Amendment XX (1933)

### Section 1

The terms of the President and Vice President shall end at noon on the 20th day of January, and the terms of Senators and Representatives at noon on the 3d day of January, of the years in which such terms would have ended if this article had not been ratified; and the terms of their successors shall then begin.

### Section 2

The Congress shall assemble at least once in every year, and such meeting shall begin at noon on the 3d day of January, unless they shall by law appoint a different day.

## Section 3

If, at the time fixed for the beginning of the term of the President, the President elect shall have died, the Vice President elect shall become President. If a President shall not have been chosen before the time fixed for the beginning of his term, or if the President elect shall have failed to qualify, then the Vice President elect shall act as President until a President shall have qualified; and the Congress may by law provide for the case wherein neither a President elect nor a Vice President elect shall have qualified, declaring who shall then act as President, or the manner in which one who is to act shall be selected, and such person shall act accordingly until a President or Vice President shall have qualified.

## Section 4

The Congress may by law provide for the case of the death of any of the persons from whom the House of Representatives may choose a President whenever the right of choice shall have devolved upon them, and for the case of the death of any of the persons from whom the Senate may choose a Vice President whenever the right of choice shall have devolved upon them.

## Section 5

Sections 1 and 2 shall take effect on the 15th day of October following the ratification of this article

### Section 6

This article shall be inoperative unless it shall have been ratified as an amendment to the Constitution by the legislatures of three-fourths of the several States within seven years from the date of its submission.

### Amendment XXI (1933)

## Section 1

The eighteenth article of amendment to the Constitution of the United States is hereby repealed.

## Section 2

The transportation or importation into any State, Territory, or possession of the United States for delivery or use therein of intoxicating liquors, in violation of the laws thereof, is hereby prohibited.

## Section 3

This article shall be inoperative unless it shall have been ratified as an amendment to the Constitution by conventions in the several States, as provided in the Constitution, within seven years from the date of the submission hereof to the States by the Congress.

### Amendment XXII (1951)

## Section 1

No person shall be elected to the office of the President more than twice, and no person who has held the office of President, or acted as President, for more than two years of a term to which some other person was elected President shall be elected to the office of the President more than once. But this Article shall not apply to any person holding the office of President, when this Article was proposed by the Congress, and shall not prevent any person who may be holding the office of President, or acting as President, during the term within which this Article becomes operative from holding the office of President or acting as President during the remainder of such term.

## Section 2

This article shall be inoperative unless it shall have been ratified as an amendment to the Constitution by the legislatures of three-fourths of the several States within seven years from the date of its submission to the States by the Congress.

### Amendment XXIII (1961)

## Section 1

The District constituting the seat of Government of the United States shall appoint in such manner as the Congress may direct:

A number of electors of President and Vice President equal to the whole number of Senators and Representatives in Congress to which the District would be entitled if it were a State, but in no event more than the least populous State; they shall be in addition to those appointed by the States, but they shall be considered, for the purposes of the election of President and Vice President, to be electors appointed by a State; and they shall meet in the District and perform such duties as provided by the twelfth article of amendment.

## Section 2

The Congress shall have power to enforce this article by appropriate legislation.

## Amendment XXIV (1964)

## Section 1

The right of citizens of the United States to vote in any primary or other election for President or Vice President for electors for President or Vice President, or for Senator or Representative in Congress, shall not be denied or abridged by the United States or any State by reason of failure to pay any poll tax or other tax.

## Section 2

The Congress shall have power to enforce this article by appropriate legislation.

## Amendment XXV (1967)

## Section 1

In case of the removal of the President from office or of his death or resignation, the Vice President shall become President.

## Section 2

Whenever there is a vacancy in the office of the Vice President, the President shall nominate a Vice President who shall take office upon confirmation by a majority vote of both Houses of Congress.

## Section 3

Whenever the President transmits to the President pro tempore of the Senate and the Speaker of the House of Representatives his written declaration that he is unable to discharge the powers and duties of his office, and until he transmits to them a written declaration to the contrary, such powers and duties shall be discharged by the Vice President as Acting President.

## Section 4

Whenever the Vice President and a majority of either the principal officers of the executive departments or of such other body as Congress may by law provide, transmit to the President pro tempore of the Senate and the Speaker of the House of Representatives their written declaration that the President is unable to discharge the powers and duties of his office, the Vice President shall immediately assume the powers and duties of the office as Acting President.

Thereafter, when the President transmits to the President pro tempore of the Senate and the Speaker of the House of Representatives his written declaration that no inability exists, he shall resume the powers and duties of his office unless the Vice President and a majority of either the principal officers of the executive department or of such other body as Congress may by law provide, transmit within four days to the President pro tempore of the Senate and the Speaker of the House of Representatives their written declaration that the President is unable to discharge the powers and duties of his office. Thereupon Congress shall decide the issue, assembling within forty-eight hours for that purpose if not in session. If the Congress, within twenty-one days after receipt of the latter written declaration, or, if Congress is not in session, within twenty-one days after Congress is required to assemble, determines by two-thirds vote of both Houses that the President is unable to discharge the powers and duties of his office, the Vice President shall continue to discharge the same as Acting President; otherwise, the President shall resume the powers and duties of his office.

## Amendment **XXVI** (1971)

### Section 1

The right of citizens of the United States, who are eighteen years of age or older, to vote shall not be denied or abridged by the United States or by any State on account of age.

### Section 2

The Congress shall have power to enforce this article by appropriate legislation.

## Amendment **XXVII** (1992)

No law varying the compensation for the services of the Senators and Representatives shall take effect, until an election of Representatives shall have intervened.

# References


The United States Constitution

The Declaration of Independence

72 members of Congress have violated a law designed to prevent insider trading and stop conflicts-of-interest by *Dave Levinthal, Insider.* updated Oct 12, 2022

'I don't plan to vote ever again': The psychology of why so many people don't vote, even in 2020 by Catherine Clifford. Published Fri, Oct 30, 2020, 9:01 AM EDT

Holy Bible, King James Version

National Archives, Declaration of Independence

National Constitution Center

The First Amendment Encyclopedia

Sheridan, Is Social Media the 21st Century's Version of Yellow Journalism

Biden vows to combat 'venom and violence' of white supremacy, The Guardian Sept. 2022

Merriam Webster Dictionary

Thumbs down on 'woke': 'Disney debacle' lesson for CEOs, by Charles Gasparino

CleanTechnica Green New Deal

John Gramlich, *gap* between the number of blacks and whites in prison is shrinking, Pew Research Center

Prison Policy Initiative

Analysis and Interpretation of the U.S. Constitution, Constitution Annotated

Cambridge Dictionary

State of Texas Constitution

Senator Robert Byrd and the Ku Klux Klan by Robert Longley. ThoughtCo.

Joe Biden embraced segregation in 1975, claiming it was a matter of "black pride", by Alana Goodman, Washington Examiner

Trump met with white supremacist Nick Fuentes alongside ye and Mar-A-Lago by Zach Schoenfeld, thehill.com

The Impact of Sea-Level Rise and Climate Change on Pacific Ocean Tolls by Pacific Coastal and Marine Science Center. USCG

U.S. Military Faces Biggest Recruiting Hurdles in 50 Years (1), by Roxana Tron, Bloomberg Government

U.S. Department of Housing and Urban Development

South Carolina veterans make up 9.2 percent of state's population, study finds, *The Center Square*